C000301367

RETRO
Baking

THE AUSTRALIAN
Women's Weekly
RETRO
Baking

COLUMBIA
COLUMBIA

Contents

Then &
NOW
Baking is back in fashion in a
big way, and home bakers are
cooking up a storm with the level
of excellence and expectation
rising to a high standard.

Retro and baking are words that just naturally go together. They capture the essence of a time when an entire day was devoted to filling the tin with baked goodies.

THE GOOD OLD RECIPES THAT WERE MADE IN HOME KITCHENS SEVERAL GENERATIONS AGO ARE AS POPULAR TODAY AS THEY WERE BACK THEN. THE RECIPES MIGHT *have been modernised* IN SOME WAY, BUT THE BASIC PROPORTIONS OF INGREDIENTS REMAIN SIMILAR. WHILE THERE ARE LIMITS TO HOW FAR THESE PROPORTIONS CAN BE PUSHED, THE TEAM IN THE TEST KITCHEN TAKE GREAT DELIGHT IN SEEING HOW FAR THEY CAN EXTEND THE BOUNDARIES AT TESTING TIME.

It's necessary to follow tried and trusted recipes – The Weekly's are all triple-tested, at least – especially when it comes to baking. It's vital to know your oven, only observation and practice will achieve this.

IT'S A SMART **BAKER** who keeps notes for future reference. Accurate scales and measuring cups and spoons are vital for success, along with using the correct sized cake pans, pie dishes etc, usually price is a guide to quality when it comes to bakeware.

MANY A *wonderful cake* OR DESSERT HAS BEEN CREATED BY CHEFS, PASTRY CHEFS AND HOME COOKS BY *making a mistake*.

Baking skills can be learned, but the best lessons of all come with practice and repetition. Never be put off by other people's stories of failure as they probably took a few liberties with a recipe. The science and **CHEMISTRY OF BAKING** is complex and mostly understood completely by experts in this field. It's enough for the home baker to understand and adhere to some simple rules and principles.

THERE IS A WONDERFUL ARRAY OF RECIPES IN THIS BOOK, SOME PERFECT FOR THE FAMILY, SCHOOL LUNCHBOXES, OTHERS QUITE DRESSED UP FOR *Special occasions* AND OF COURSE EVERYTHING IN BETWEEN. ENJOY WITH US, THE WONDERFUL WORLD OF BAKING.

PIES
& PASTRIES

MINI CHERRY BAKEWELL TARTS

PREP + COOK TIME 1 HOUR (+ REFRIGERATION & COOLING) **MAKES** 24

90G (3 OUNCES) UNSALTED BUTTER, SOFTENED
2 TABLESPOONS CASTER (SUPERFINE) SUGAR
1 EGG YOLK
1 CUP (150G) PLAIN (ALL-PURPOSE) FLOUR
½ CUP (60G) GROUND ALMONDS
2 TABLESPOONS STRAWBERRY JAM
12 RED GLACÉ CHERRIES, HALVED

ALMOND FILLING

125G (4 OUNCES) UNSALTED BUTTER, SOFTENED
½ TEASPOON FINELY GRATED LEMON RIND
½ CUP (110G) CASTER (SUPERFINE) SUGAR
2 EGGS
¾ CUP (90G) GROUND ALMONDS
2 TABLESPOONS PLAIN (ALL-PURPOSE) FLOUR

LEMON GLAZE

1 CUP (160G) ICING (CONFECTIONERS') SUGAR
2 TABLESPOONS LEMON JUICE, APPROXIMATELY

1 Beat butter, sugar and egg yolk in a small bowl with an electric mixer until combined. Stir in sifted flour and ground almonds, in two batches. Knead dough on a floured surface until smooth. Wrap pastry in plastic wrap; refrigerate 30 minutes.
2 Preheat oven to 200°C/400°F. Grease two 12-hole (1½-tablespoon/30ml) shallow round-based patty pans.
3 Make almond filling.
4 Roll pastry between sheets of baking paper until 3mm (⅛-inch) thick. Cut 24 x 6cm (2¼-inch) rounds from pastry; gently press rounds into pan holes. Divide jam then filling into cases.
5 Bake tarts for 20 minutes. Leave tarts in pans for 10 minutes before turning, top-side up, onto a wire rack.
6 Meanwhile, make lemon glaze.
7 Spoon glaze over warm tarts; top with cherries. Cool.

almond filling Beat butter, rind and sugar in a small bowl with an electric mixer until light and fluffy. Beat in eggs, one at a time. Stir in ground almonds and flour.

lemon glaze Sift icing sugar into a small bowl, stir in enough juice to make glaze pourable.

LEMON MERINGUE PIE

PREP + COOK TIME 1 HOUR 10 MINUTES (+ REFRIGERATION) **SERVES** 10

½ CUP (75G) CORNFLOUR (CORNSTARCH)
1 CUP (220G) CASTER (SUPERFINE) SUGAR
½ CUP (125ML) LEMON JUICE
1¼ CUPS (310ML) WATER
2 TEASPOONS FINELY GRATED LEMON RIND
60G (2 OUNCES) UNSALTED BUTTER, CHOPPED
3 EGGS, SEPARATED
⅓ CUP (150G) CASTER (SUPERFINE) SUGAR, EXTRA

PASTRY

1½ CUPS (225G) PLAIN (ALL-PURPOSE) FLOUR
1 TABLESPOON ICING (CONFECTIONERS') SUGAR
140G (4½ OUNCES) COLD BUTTER, CHOPPED
1 EGG, SEPARATED (SEE TIPS)
2 TABLESPOONS COLD WATER

1 Make pastry.

2 Grease a 24cm (9½-inch) round loose-based fluted flan tin. Roll pastry between sheets of baking paper until large enough to line tin. Ease pastry into tin, press into base and side; trim edge. Cover; refrigerate 30 minutes.

3 Preheat oven to 200°C/400°F.

4 Place tin on an oven tray. Line pastry case with baking paper; fill with dried beans or rice. Bake 15 minutes. Remove paper and beans; bake for 10 minutes. Cool; turn oven off.

5 Meanwhile, combine cornflour and sugar in a medium saucepan. Gradually stir in juice and the water until smooth; cook, stirring, until mixture boils and thickens. Reduce heat; simmer, stirring, 1 minute. Remove from heat; stir in rind, butter and egg yolks. Cool 10 minutes.

6 Spread filling into pie shell. Cover; refrigerate 2 hours.

7 Preheat oven to 240°C/475°F.

8 Beat egg whites (including the reserved egg white from the pastry) in a small bowl with an electric mixer until soft peaks form; gradually add extra sugar, beating until sugar dissolves.

9 Roughen surface of filling with a fork before spreading with meringue mixture. Bake pie for 2 minutes or until meringue is browned lightly.

pastry Process flour, sugar and butter until crumbly. Add egg yolk and the water; process until ingredients come together. Knead dough on a floured surface until smooth. Wrap pastry in plastic wrap; refrigerate 30 minutes.

tips In the pastry, you only need to use the egg yolk; reserve the egg white and add it to the meringue mixture in step 8. This pie is best eaten on the day it is made.

RASPBERRY ALMOND CRUMBLE TART

PREP + COOK TIME 1 HOUR (+ REFRIGERATION & COOLING) **SERVES** 8

1½ CUPS (225G) FROZEN RASPBERRIES
1 TEASPOON ICING (CONFECTIONERS') SUGAR

ALMOND PASTRY

150G (4½ OUNCES) BUTTER, SOFTENED
1 TEASPOON VANILLA EXTRACT
⅔ CUP (150G) CASTER (SUPERFINE) SUGAR
1 EGG
½ CUP (60G) GROUND ALMONDS
1½ CUPS (225G) PLAIN (ALL-PURPOSE) FLOUR

1 Make almond pastry.
2 Roll two-thirds of the pastry between sheets of baking paper until large enough to line an 11cm x 35cm (4½-inch x 14-inch) rectangular loose-based flan tin. Ease pastry into tin, press into base and sides; trim edges. Prick pastry base with a fork; refrigerate 30 minutes. Crumble remaining pastry; reserve.
3 Preheat oven to 200°C/400°F.
4 Place flan tin on an oven tray; bake 10 minutes or until browned lightly. Sprinkle raspberries over base; top with reserved crumbled pastry. Bake a further 20 minutes or until browned. Cool in pan. Dust with icing sugar before serving.

almond pastry Beat butter in a small bowl with an electric mixer until smooth. Add extract, sugar and egg; beat until combined. Stir in ground almonds and half the flour. Work in remaining flour using your hands. Knead pastry on a floured surface until smooth. Wrap pastry in plastic wrap; refrigerate 30 minutes.
tip This recipe is best made on the day of serving as the raspberries will soften the pastry.
serving suggestion Serve with thick (double) cream, custard or vanilla ice-cream.

pop
COLA

CLASSIC
APPLE PIE

PREP + COOK TIME 1¾ HOURS (+ REFRIGERATION) **SERVES** 8

10 MEDIUM APPLES (1.5KG)
½ CUP (125ML) WATER
¼ CUP (55G) CASTER (SUPERFINE) SUGAR
1 TEASPOON FINELY GRATED LEMON RIND
¼ TEASPOON GROUND CINNAMON
1 EGG WHITE
1 TABLESPOON CASTER (SUPERFINE) SUGAR, EXTRA

PASTRY

1 CUP (150G) PLAIN (ALL-PURPOSE) FLOUR
½ CUP (75G) SELF-RAISING FLOUR
¼ CUP (35G) CORNFLOUR (CORNSTARCH)
¼ CUP (30G) CUSTARD POWDER
1 TABLESPOON CASTER (SUPERFINE) SUGAR
100G (3 OUNCES) COLD BUTTER, CHOPPED COARSELY
1 EGG YOLK
¼ CUP (60ML) ICED WATER

1 Make pastry.

2 Peel, core and slice apples thickly. Place apples and the water in a large saucepan; bring to the boil. Reduce heat; simmer, covered, for 10 minutes or until apples soften. Drain; stir in sugar, rind and cinnamon. Cool.

3 Preheat oven to 220°C/425°F. Grease a deep 25cm (10-inch) pie dish.

4 Divide pastry in half. Roll one half between sheets of baking paper until large enough to line dish. Lift pastry into dish; press into base and side. Spoon apple mixture into pastry case; brush edge with egg white.

5 Roll remaining pastry until large enough to cover filling; lift onto filling. Press edges together; trim away excess pastry. Brush pastry with egg white; sprinkle with extra sugar.

6 Bake pie for 20 minutes. Reduce oven to 180°C/350°F; bake for a further 25 minutes or until golden brown.

pastry Process dry ingredients with butter until crumbly. Add egg yolk and the water; process until combined. Knead on a floured surface until smooth. Wrap in plastic wrap; refrigerate 30 minutes.

tips Make sure the apple filling has drained well and cooled to room temperature before you add it to the pastry case. Brushing the pastry case first with a little of the egg white before you add the filling will also help stop the apples from making the pastry soggy.

OLD-FASHIONED APPLE & RHUBARB PIE

PREP + COOK TIME 2 HOURS (+ COOLING & REFRIGERATION) **SERVES** 8

5 LARGE APPLES (1KG), PEELED, SLICED THICKLY
⅓ CUP (75G) CASTER (SUPERFINE) SUGAR
½ CUP (125ML) WATER
1 VANILLA BEAN, SPLIT LENGTHWAYS
500G (1 POUND) TRIMMED RHUBARB, CHOPPED COARSELY
1 TABLESPOON LEMON JUICE
1 EGG, BEATEN LIGHTLY
1 TEASPOON WHITE (GRANULATED) SUGAR

ALMOND PASTRY

2½ CUPS (375G) PLAIN (ALL-PURPOSE) FLOUR
½ CUP (60G) GROUND ALMONDS
1 CUP (160G) ICING (CONFECTIONERS') SUGAR
250G (8 OUNCES) COLD BUTTER, CHOPPED COARSELY
2 EGG YOLKS
1 TABLESPOON ICED WATER

1 Combine apple, caster sugar, the water and one half of the vanilla bean in a large saucepan, cover; bring to the boil. Reduce heat; simmer for 10 minutes or until apple is tender. Stir in rhubarb, cover; simmer for 3 minutes or until rhubarb is soft. Drain well. Transfer apple mixture to a medium bowl; stir in juice. Cool.

2 Make almond pastry.

3 Preheat oven to 180°C/350°F.

4 Roll two-thirds of the pastry between sheets of baking paper until large enough to line a deep 24cm (9½-inch) pie dish. Lift pastry into dish; press into base and side, trim edge then pinch pastry. Refrigerate 30 minutes.

5 Line pastry with baking paper; fill with dried beans or rice. Place on an oven tray; bake 15 minutes. Remove paper and beans; bake a further 15 minutes or until browned. Cool.

6 Spoon apple mixture into pastry case. Roll remaining pastry between sheets of baking paper until large enough to cover pie dish. Brush edge of pastry case with a little of the egg. Place pastry over pie; trim edge, then pinch pastry. Cut out a 2.5cm (1-inch) round from centre of pie. Brush pastry with a little more egg; sprinkle with white sugar.

7 Bake pie for 35 minutes or until browned. Stand 10 minutes before serving.

almond pastry Scrape seeds from remaining half of vanilla bean. Process flour, ground almonds, icing sugar and butter until crumbly. Add egg yolks, vanilla seeds and enough of the water, processing until ingredients just come together. Knead dough on a floured surface until smooth. Wrap pastry in plastic wrap; refrigerate 30 minutes.

PASSIONFRUIT CURD & COCONUT TARTS

PREP + COOK TIME 1¼ HOURS (+ COOLING & REFRIGERATION) **MAKES** 12

1 CUP (80G) DESICCATED COCONUT
1 EGG WHITE, BEATEN LIGHTLY
2 TABLESPOONS CASTER (SUPERFINE) SUGAR
¼ CUP (60ML) THICKENED (HEAVY) CREAM
1 TABLESPOON PASSIONFRUIT PULP

PASSIONFRUIT CURD

½ CUP (125ML) PASSIONFRUIT PULP
½ TEASPOON FINELY GRATED LEMON RIND
1 TABLESPOON LEMON JUICE
½ CUP (110G) CASTER (SUPERFINE) SUGAR
80G (2½ OUNCES) BUTTER, CHOPPED COARSELY
1 EGG, BEATEN LIGHTLY
1 EGG YOLK

1 Make passionfruit curd.
2 Preheat oven to 150°C/300°F. Grease a 12-hole (1-tablespoon/20ml) mini muffin pan.
3 Combine coconut, egg white and sugar in a small bowl. Press mixture firmly and evenly over base and side of pan holes.
4 Bake tart cases for 20 minutes or until browned lightly around the edges. Cool in pan.
5 Meanwhile, beat cream in a small bowl with an electric mixer until firm peaks form; fold into ½ cup of the passionfruit curd. (Store remaining curd for another use, see tips.)
6 Transfer coconut cases to a serving plate; spoon passionfruit curd mixture into cases. Top each tart with a little passionfruit pulp.

passionfruit curd Press passionfruit pulp firmly through a sieve over a small bowl. You will need ¼ cup passionfruit juice for this recipe. Discard seeds. Combine passionfruit juice with remaining ingredients in a medium heatproof bowl; stir over a medium saucepan of simmering water for 10 minutes or until mixture thickly coats the back of a wooden spoon. Cool. Refrigerate 2 hours or until cold.

tips You will need about 6 passionfruit for this recipe. Remaining passionfruit curd is delicious spread on scones or used as a filling for pavlovas. These tarts are best made on the day of serving.

MIXED BERRY & RICOTTA TART

PREP + COOK TIME 1½ HOURS (+ REFRIGERATION) **SERVES** 10

1⅓ CUPS (200G) PLAIN (ALL-PURPOSE) FLOUR
185G (6 OUNCES) COLD BUTTER, CHOPPED COARSELY
¼ CUP (60ML) ICED WATER, APPROXIMATELY
500G (1 POUND) SOFT RICOTTA
⅓ CUP (80ML) POURING CREAM
⅓ CUP (75G) CASTER (SUPERFINE) SUGAR
3 EGGS
1 TABLESPOON FINELY GRATED LEMON RIND
200G (6½ OUNCES) STRAWBERRIES, HALVED
125G (4 OUNCES) BLUEBERRIES
125G (4 OUNCES) RASPBERRIES
2 TEASPOONS ICING (CONFECTIONERS') SUGAR

1 Sift flour into a large bowl; rub in butter until crumbly. Mix in enough of the water to make ingredients just come together. Knead dough gently on a floured surface until smooth. Flatten pastry slightly, wrap in plastic wrap; refrigerate 30 minutes.
2 Grease a 22cm (9-inch) round loose-based fluted flan tin. Roll out pastry between sheets of baking paper until large enough to line tin. Ease pastry into tin, press into base and side; trim edge. Prick base all over with a fork; refrigerate 30 minutes.
3 Preheat oven to 200°C/400°F.
4 Place tin on an oven tray. Line pastry with baking paper; fill with dried beans or rice. Bake for 15 minutes. Remove paper and beans; bake a further 10 minutes or until browned lightly and crisp. Cool.
5 Reduce oven to 180°C/350°F.
6 Meanwhile, beat ricotta, cream, caster sugar, eggs and rind in a small bowl with an electric mixer until smooth. Pour mixture into tart shell.
7 Bake tart for 35 minutes or until filling is just set. Refrigerate until cold. Just before serving, top tart with berries; dust with sifted icing sugar.

tips You can also make the pastry using a food processor. Process flour and butter until crumbly; with motor operating, add the water and process until ingredients just come together. You could also use ready-made shortcrust pastry. This tart is best made on the day of serving.

QUINCE & RHUBARB PIE

PREP + COOK TIME 3 HOURS (+ REFRIGERATION) **SERVES** 8

2 CUPS (500ML) WATER
2 CUPS (440G) CASTER (SUPERFINE) SUGAR
4 MEDIUM QUINCE (1.2KG), PEELED, QUARTERED
2 STRIPS LEMON RIND
500G (1 POUND) RHUBARB, CHOPPED COARSELY
¼ CUP (60ML) LEMON JUICE, APPROXIMATELY
1 CUP (150G) PLAIN (ALL-PURPOSE) FLOUR
⅓ CUP (55G) ICING (CONFECTIONERS') SUGAR
100G (3 OUNCES) COLD BUTTER, CHOPPED
1 EGG, SEPARATED
1 TABLESPOON ICED WATER, APPROXIMATELY
1 TABLESPOON RAW SUGAR

1 Stir the water and sugar in a medium saucepan over low heat until sugar has dissolved. Add quince and rind; bring to the boil. Reduce heat; simmer, covered, for 2 hours or until quince is tender and a rosy colour. Add rhubarb; cook for 5 minutes or until rhubarb softens. Add juice to taste, to reduce sweetness. Cool quince and rhubarb in the syrup.

2 Meanwhile, process flour, icing sugar and butter until crumbly. Add egg yolk and iced water, process until ingredients just come together. Knead dough gently on floured surface until smooth. Cover; refrigerate 30 minutes.

3 Preheat oven to 180°C/350°F. Grease a 23cm (9¼-inch) pie dish.

4 Drain fruit mixture, reserving ⅓ cup of the syrup. Spoon fruit mixture and reserved syrup into dish.

5 Roll out pastry until large enough to cover pie. Using a 1cm (½-inch) cutter, cut out rounds from pastry, reserving rounds. Place pastry over filling; trim edge. Place rounds on pastry, brush a little of the lightly beaten egg white over pastry; sprinkle with raw sugar. Place pie on an oven tray.

6 Bake pie for 30 minutes or until well browned. (Cover the edges of the pastry with foil after 20 minutes to prevent over-browning.) Stand 10 minutes before serving.

serving suggestion Serve with thick (double) cream.

BANOFFEE PIE

PREP + COOK TIME 1 HOUR (+ REFRIGERATION & STANDING) **SERVES** 8

2 X 395G (12½ OUNCES) CANNED SWEETENED CONDENSED MILK
150G (4½ OUNCES) BUTTER, CHOPPED
1 CUP (220G) FIRMLY PACKED BROWN SUGAR
⅓ CUP (115G) GOLDEN SYRUP
2 LARGE BANANAS (460G), SLICED THINLY
300ML THICKENED (HEAVY) CREAM, WHIPPED

PASTRY

1½ CUPS (225G) PLAIN (ALL-PURPOSE) FLOUR
1 TABLESPOON ICING (CONFECTIONERS') SUGAR
140G (4½ OUNCES) COLD BUTTER, CHOPPED
1 EGG YOLK
2 TABLESPOONS COLD WATER

1 Make pastry.
2 Grease a 24cm (9½-inch) round loose-based fluted flan tin. Roll pastry between sheets of baking paper until large enough to line tin. Ease pastry into tin; press into base and side. Trim edge; prick base all over with a fork. Cover; refrigerate 30 minutes.
3 Preheat oven to 200°C/400°F.
4 Place tin on an oven tray; line pastry with baking paper, fill with dried beans or rice. Bake 10 minutes. Carefully remove paper and beans; bake for a further 10 minutes. Cool.
5 Meanwhile, place condensed milk, butter, sugar and syrup in a medium saucepan over medium heat, stirring continuously, for 16 minutes or until mixture is caramel-coloured. Stand for 5 minutes.
6 Pour filling into cooled pastry case; cool. Just before serving, arrange banana slices on caramel and top with cream. Sprinkle with ground nutmeg, if you like.

pastry Process flour, sugar and butter until crumbly; add egg yolk and the water, process until ingredients come together. Knead dough on floured surface until smooth. Wrap in plastic wrap; refrigerate 30 minutes.

BERRY & RHUBARB MINI PIES

PREP + COOK TIME 1 HOUR (+ REFRIGERATION) **MAKES** 6

2 CUPS (220G) COARSELY CHOPPED RHUBARB
¼ CUP (55G) CASTER (SUPERFINE) SUGAR
2 TABLESPOONS WATER
1 TABLESPOON CORNFLOUR (CORNSTARCH)
2 CUPS (300G) FROZEN MIXED BERRIES
1 EGG, BEATEN LIGHTLY
2 TEASPOONS DEMERARA SUGAR

PASTRY

1⅔ CUPS (250G) PLAIN (ALL-PURPOSE) FLOUR
⅓ CUP (75G) CASTER (SUPERFINE) SUGAR
150G (4½ OUNCES) COLD BUTTER, CHOPPED COARSELY
1 EGG YOLK
2 TEASPOONS WATER

1 Make pastry.

2 Place rhubarb, caster sugar and half the water in a medium saucepan; bring to the boil. Reduce heat; simmer, covered, for 3 minutes or until rhubarb is tender. Blend cornflour with the remaining water; stir into rhubarb mixture. Stir over heat until mixture boils and thickens. Remove from heat; stir in berries. Cool.

3 Grease six 12.5cm (5-inch) pie tins (top measure) (¾-cup/180ml). Roll two-thirds of the pastry between sheets of baking paper until 4mm (¼ inch) thick. Cut out six 12cm (4¾-inch) rounds; press rounds into base and side of tins. Refrigerate 30 minutes.

4 Preheat oven to 200°C/400°F.

5 Roll remaining pastry between sheets of baking paper until 4mm (¼ inch) thick; cut out six 9cm (3¾-inch) rounds.

6 Spoon fruit mixture into pastry cases.

7 Brush edge of 9cm (3¾-inch) rounds with a little of the egg; place over filling. Press edges firmly to seal. Brush tops with a little more egg; sprinkle with demerara sugar.

8 Bake pies about 30 minutes. Leave in tins for 10 minutes. Using a palette knife, loosen pies from edge of pan before lifting out.

pastry Process flour, sugar and butter until crumbly. Add egg yolk and the water; process until combined. Knead on a floured surface until smooth. Wrap dough in plastic wrap; refrigerate 30 minutes.

tips You need 4 large stems of rhubarb for this recipe. If you don't have pie tins, you could use a 6-hole (¾-cup/180ml) texas muffin pan instead. For other pie decorating ideas, see pages 32 & 33.

serving suggestion Serve warm with vanilla ice-cream.

BEADED EDGE

USING A FLOURED 2.5CM (1-INCH) ROUND CUTTER, CUT OUT ENOUGH ROUNDS FROM SHORTCRUST PASTRY. BRUSH A LITTLE WATER ON THE EDGE OF THE PIE, THEN POSITION EACH ROUND ON THE PIE EDGE, OVERLAPPING SLIGHTLY, UNTIL THE EDGE IS COVERED.

TWISTED SPIRAL TOP

USING A FLOURED PASTRY WHEEL, CUT NARROW STRIPS OF SHORTCRUST PASTRY. POSITION ON PIE IN A ZIGZAG PATTERN; BRUSH PIE EDGE WITH WATER TO SECURE.

Decorating PIES

LATTICE TOP

USING A FLOURED PASTRY WHEEL, CUT SHORTCRUST PASTRY INTO NARROW STRIPS. WITHOUT STRETCHING THE PASTRY, "WEAVE" THE PASTRY STRIPS DIRECTLY OVER THE PIE FILLING; TRIM THE EDGE, BRUSH WITH A LITTLE WATER TO HOLD LATTICE STRIPS IN POSITION.

CUT-OUTS

CUTTING SHAPES OUT OF PASTRY NOT ONLY LOOKS GOOD IT ALSO ALLOWS STEAM TO ESCAPE FROM THE PIE. USING ANY SIZE AND SHAPE OF COOKIE CUTTER YOU LIKE, DIP THE CUTTER IN FLOUR; SHAKE OFF EXCESS, CUT OUT THE SHAPES FROM SHORTCRUST OR PUFF PASTRY BEFORE THE PASTRY IS PLACED OVER THE FILLING. CRIMP THE EDGE OF THE PIE WITH A FORK TO SEAL.

APRICOT & ALMOND JALOUSIE

PREP + COOK TIME 35 MINUTES (+ STANDING) **SERVES** 8

375G (12-OUNCE) PACKET PUFF PASTRY
1 TABLESPOON APRICOT JAM, WARMED
1 EGG WHITE
2 TEASPOONS CASTER (SUPERFINE) SUGAR

ALMOND FILLING

30G (1 OUNCE) BUTTER
1 CUP (80G) FLAKED ALMONDS
2 TABLESPOONS CASTER (SUPERFINE) SUGAR
1 TEASPOON VANILLA EXTRACT
2 EGG YOLKS
2 TEASPOONS PLAIN (ALL-PURPOSE) FLOUR

1 Make almond filling.
2 Preheat oven to 220°C/425°F.
3 Cut pastry in half. Roll one half into a neatly trimmed 12cm x 25cm (4¾-inch x 10-inch) rectangle; place on an oven tray. Spread sieved jam over centre. Place almond filling on pastry leaving a 2cm (¾-inch) border around the edge.
4 Roll remaining pastry into a neatly trimmed 13cm x 27cm (5¼-inch x 10¾-inch) rectangle; fold in half lengthways. Brush pastry on both sides with egg white. Cut through folded edge of pastry at 2cm (¾-inch) intervals leaving a 2cm (¾-inch) border down long side of pastry strip.
5 Brush around edge of pastry strip on oven tray with egg white. Carefully unfold cut pastry strip, place over almond filling. Press edges of pastry together using your thumb and the back of a knife to make a decorative edge. Brush evenly with egg white; sprinkle with sugar.
6 Bake jalousie for 5 minutes. Reduce oven to 200°C/400°F; bake for a further 10 minutes or until golden brown.
almond filling Melt butter in a small saucepan, add almonds; cook, stirring constantly, over heat until browned lightly. Process almond mixture with remaining ingredients until smooth.
tip Jalousie is best made on the day of serving.

CHOUQUETTES (SUGAR PUFFS)

PREP + COOK TIME 40 MINUTES **MAKES** 40

½ CUP (125ML) WATER
60G (2 OUNCES) BUTTER
1 TABLESPOON CASTER (SUPERFINE) SUGAR
½ CUP (75G) BAKER'S FLOUR
4 EGGS
¼ CUP (45G) PEARL SUGAR

1 Preheat oven to 220°C/425°F. Grease oven trays.
2 Combine the water, butter and caster sugar in a small saucepan; bring to the boil. Add flour; beat with a wooden spoon over medium heat until the mixture comes away from the base of the pan. Transfer choux pastry to a medium bowl; beat in three of the eggs, one at a time, until pastry becomes smooth and glossy but still holds its shape.
3 Spoon pastry into piping bag fitted with a 1cm (½-inch) plain tube. Pipe small rounds, about 5cm (2 inches) apart, on trays; brush all over with lightly beaten remaining egg, sprinkle with pearl sugar.
4 Bake puffs for 20 minutes or until golden and puffed. Serve warm.

tips These puffs are best eaten soon after baking. They are a traditional French afternoon snack for kids after school. They are sold at bakeries by the weight in paper bags. Pearl sugar is a coarse white sugar that keeps its shape when heated or exposed to moisture; it is available from specialist food stores and cake decorating suppliers.

CLASSIC PUFFS

PREP + COOK TIME 1¼ HOURS (+ COOLING & REFRIGERATION) **MAKES** 20

½ CUP (125ML) WATER
60G (2 OUNCES) BUTTER, CHOPPED FINELY
1 TABLESPOON CASTER (SUPERFINE) SUGAR
½ CUP (75G) BAKER'S FLOUR
3 EGGS
1 TABLESPOON ICING (CONFECTIONERS') SUGAR

CRÈME PÂTISSIÈRE

3 CUPS (750ML) MILK
⅔ CUP (150G) CASTER (SUPERFINE) SUGAR
1 TEASPOON VANILLA EXTRACT
6 EGG YOLKS
⅓ CUP (50G) CORNFLOUR (CORNSTARCH)

1 Make crème pâtissière.
2 Preheat oven to 220°C/425°F. Grease oven trays.
3 Combine the water, butter and caster sugar in a medium saucepan; bring to the boil. Add flour; beat with a wooden spoon over medium heat until the mixture comes away from the base of the pan. Transfer choux pastry to a medium bowl; beat in two of the eggs, one at a time. Whisk remaining egg with a fork; beat enough of the egg into the pastry until it becomes smooth and glossy but still holds its shape.
4 Drop level tablespoons of the pastry, about 5cm (2 inches) apart, onto trays.
5 Bake puffs for 10 minutes. Reduce oven to 180°C/350°F; bake 15 minutes. Cut a small opening into the base of each puff; bake a further 10 minutes or until puffs are dry. Cool on trays.
6 Spoon crème pâtissière into a piping bag fitted with a 5mm (¼-inch) plain tube; pipe through cuts into puffs. Dust puffs with sifted icing sugar.

crème pâtissière Bring milk, sugar and extract to the boil in a medium saucepan. Meanwhile, whisk egg yolks and cornflour in a medium heatproof bowl. Gradually add hot milk mixture to egg mixture. Return mixture to pan; stir over medium heat until it boils and thickens. Cover surface with plastic wrap. Refrigerate 4 hours.

tips Crème pâtissière can be made a day ahead; store, covered, in the refrigerator. It will need to be softened before piping; beat it with an electric mixer until smooth.

CHOCOLATE MOUSSE PUFFS

PREP + COOK TIME 1 HOUR (+ REFRIGERATION) **MAKES** 32

1 CUP (250ML) WATER
80G (2½ OUNCES) BUTTER, CHOPPED COARSELY
1 CUP (150G) PLAIN (ALL-PURPOSE) FLOUR
2 TABLESPOONS COCOA POWDER
4 EGGS
2 TEASPOONS DRINKING CHOCOLATE

CHOCOLATE MOUSSE FILLING

1⅔ CUPS (250G) WHITE CHOCOLATE MELTS
600ML THICKENED (HEAVY) CREAM
125G (4 OUNCES) CREAM CHEESE, SOFTENED
⅔ CUP (150G) CASTER (SUPERFINE) SUGAR
2 EGG YOLKS

1 Make chocolate mousse filling.

2 Preheat oven to 220°C/425°F. Grease oven trays.

3 Bring the water and butter to the boil in a small saucepan. Add sifted flour and cocoa, beat with a wooden spoon over heat until mixture comes away from side of pan and forms a smooth ball.

4 Transfer mixture to a small bowl; beat in eggs, one at a time, with an electric mixer until mixture becomes glossy. Drop level tablespoons of mixture, 4cm (1½ inches) apart, onto trays.

5 Bake for 15 minutes or until pastry is puffed. Using a skewer, make a small hole in base of each puff; cool on wire racks.

6 Reduce oven to 200°C/400°F.

7 Split puffs in half, use a teaspoon to scoop out any uncooked mixture; return halves, cut-side up, to oven trays. Bake for 10 minutes or until puffs are crisp; cool on wire racks.

8 Just before serving, spoon mousse filling into bottom half of puffs, replace tops. Serve dusted with sifted drinking chocolate.

chocolate mousse filling Stir chocolate in a small heatproof bowl over a small saucepan of simmering water until melted. Beat cream in a medium bowl with an electric mixer until soft peaks form. Beat cream cheese, sugar and egg yolks in a large bowl with electric mixer until smooth. Just before the melted chocolate sets, beat into cheese mixture then fold in cream, in two batches. Cover; refrigerate until cold.

tip Unfilled puffs and chocolate mousse filling can be made a day ahead; assemble no more than an hour before serving.

CARAMEL ÉCLAIRS

PREP + COOK TIME 2¼ HOURS (+ COOLING) **MAKES** 18

395G (12½ OUNCES) CANNED SWEETENED CONDENSED MILK
½ CUP (125ML) WATER
60G (2 OUNCES) BUTTER, CHOPPED FINELY
1 TABLESPOON DARK BROWN SUGAR
½ CUP (75G) BAKER'S FLOUR
3 EGGS
2 CUPS (500ML) THICKENED (HEAVY) CREAM

CARAMEL ICING

30G (1 OUNCE) BUTTER, CHOPPED COARSELY
¼ CUP (55G) FIRMLY PACKED DARK BROWN SUGAR
1 TABLESPOON MILK
⅓ CUP (55G) ICING (CONFECTIONERS') SUGAR

1 Preheat oven to 220°C/425°F.

2 Pour condensed milk into a medium shallow baking dish; cover with foil. Place dish in a large baking dish; add enough boiling water to large dish to come halfway up sides of dish. Transfer to oven; bake, uncovered, for 1¼ hours or until condensed milk is golden brown and caramel. Cool to room temperature. Whisk caramel until smooth.

3 Combine the water, butter and brown sugar in a medium saucepan; bring to the boil. Add flour; beat with a wooden spoon over medium heat until mixture comes away from the base of the pan. Transfer choux pastry to a medium bowl; beat in two of the eggs, one at a time. Whisk remaining egg with a fork, beat enough of the egg into the pastry until it becomes smooth and glossy but still holds its shape.

4 Spoon pastry into a piping bag fitted with a 1.5cm (¾-inch) plain tube. Pipe 8cm (3-inch) lengths, about 5cm (2 inches) apart, on greased oven trays.

5 Bake éclairs for 10 minutes. Reduce oven to 180°C/350°F; bake for 15 minutes. Using a serrated knife, cut éclairs in half, remove any soft centres; return to trays, bake a further 5 minutes or until éclairs are dry. Cool on trays.

6 Meanwhile, make caramel icing.

7 Beat cream in a small bowl with an electric mixer until firm peaks form.

8 Spread caramel into éclair bases; top with whipped cream. Position éclair tops on cream; spread with caramel icing.

caramel icing Melt butter in a small saucepan, add brown sugar and milk; cook, stirring, over high heat, without boiling, until sugar dissolves. Bring to the boil. Reduce heat; simmer, uncovered, for 1 minute. Remove from heat; cool 10 minutes. Whisk in sifted icing sugar. (If the icing becomes too thick, stir in 2 teaspoons boiling water for a better consistency.)

COCONUT PUFFS

PREP + COOK TIME 1 HOUR (+ COOLING) MAKES 18

⅔ CUP (160ML) WATER
50G (1½ OUNCES) BUTTER, CHOPPED FINELY
1 TABLESPOON CASTER (SUPERFINE) SUGAR
⅔ CUP (100G) BAKER'S FLOUR
3 EGGS
150G (4½ OUNCES) WHITE CHOCOLATE MELTS
½ CUP (35G) MOIST COCONUT FLAKES

COCONUT PASTRY CREAM

2 CUPS (500ML) MILK
5 EGG YOLKS
½ CUP (110G) CASTER (SUPERFINE) SUGAR
¼ CUP (35G) CORNFLOUR (CORNSTARCH)
2 TABLESPOONS COCONUT LIQUEUR
40G (1½ OUNCES) BUTTER

1 Preheat oven to 220°C/425°F. Grease oven trays.
2 Combine the water, butter and sugar in a medium saucepan; bring to the boil. Add flour; beat with a wooden spoon over medium heat until mixture comes away from the base of the pan. Transfer choux pastry to a medium bowl; stand 1 minute. Beat in two of the eggs, one at a time, until pastry becomes smooth and glossy but still holds its shape.
3 Spoon pastry into a piping bag fitted with a 1.5cm (¾-inch) plain tube. Pipe 18 x 4cm (1½-inch) rounds, about 5cm (2-inches) apart, on trays; brush with lightly beaten remaining egg.
4 Bake puffs for 10 minutes. Reduce oven to 160°C/325°F; bake a further 20 minutes. Turn off oven; cool puffs in oven with door ajar.
5 Make coconut pastry cream.
6 Cut a small opening in base of each puff. Spoon pastry cream into piping bag fitted with an 8mm (½-inch) plain tube. Pipe pastry cream through cuts into each puff.
7 Place chocolate in a medium heatproof bowl over a medium saucepan of simmering water (make sure water doesn't touch base of bowl); stir until melted. Place coconut in a shallow dish. Dip the puffs into melted chocolate then into coconut; stand on wire racks until set.

coconut pastry cream Bring milk to the boil in a medium saucepan over medium heat. Meanwhile, whisk egg yolks, sugar and cornflour in a medium heatproof bowl. Whisk hot milk mixture into egg mixture. Return mixture to pan; whisk over medium heat until it boils and thickens. Remove from heat; whisk in liqueur and butter until smooth. Cover surface with plastic wrap. Cool to room temperature.

tips Once filled, the choux puffs will soften, so assemble 1-2 hours before eating. If making the pastry cream in advance, store, covered, in the fridge.

PARIS BREST

PREP + COOK TIME 1¼ HOURS (+ COOLING) **MAKES** 12

½ CUP (125ML) WATER
60G (2 OUNCES) BUTTER, CHOPPED FINELY
1 TABLESPOON CASTER (SUPERFINE) SUGAR
½ CUP (75G) BAKER'S FLOUR
3 EGGS
2 TABLESPOONS FLAKED ALMONDS
1 TABLESPOON ICING (CONFECTIONERS') SUGAR

PRALINE CREAM

⅓ CUP (75G) CASTER (SUPERFINE) SUGAR
2 TABLESPOONS WATER
⅓ CUP (25G) FLAKED ALMONDS, TOASTED
2 CUPS (500ML) THICKENED (HEAVY) CREAM

1 Preheat oven to 220°C/425°F. Grease oven trays.

2 Combine the water, butter and caster sugar in a medium saucepan; bring to the boil. Add flour; beat with a wooden spoon over medium heat until mixture comes away from the base of the pan. Transfer choux pastry to a medium bowl; beat in two of the eggs, one at a time. Whisk remaining egg with a fork; beat enough of the egg into the pastry until it becomes smooth and glossy but still holds its shape.

3 Spoon pastry into a piping bag fitted with a 1.5cm (¾-inch) fluted tube; pipe 5.5cm (2¼-inch) rings, about 5cm (2 inches) apart on trays. Sprinkle top with nuts.

4 Bake pastry rings for 10 minutes. Reduce oven to 180°C/350°F; bake for 15 minutes. Using a serrated knife, split rings in half, remove any soft centres; return rings to trays, bake a further 5 minutes or until puffs are dry. Cool on trays.

5 Meanwhile, make praline cream.

6 Spread cream into pastry bases; top with pastry tops. Dust with sifted icing sugar.

praline cream Line an oven tray with baking paper. Stir sugar and the water in a small saucepan over high heat, without boiling, until sugar dissolves. Bring to the boil. Boil, uncovered, without stirring, until golden brown. Allow bubbles to subside, then add nuts; do not stir. Pour mixture onto tray; leave praline to set at room temperature. Beat cream in a small bowl with an electric mixer until soft peaks form. Break praline into pieces, then process until fine; fold into whipped cream.

tips To toast nuts, place nuts, in a single layer, in a small dry frying pan; cook, over low heat, stirring often, until nuts are fragrant and just changed in colour. Remove nuts immediately from pan. This pastry, shaped like a bicycle wheel, is thought to be named after a famous bicycle race in France, between Paris and Brest, in Brittany.

VANILLA CITRUS TART

PREP + COOK TIME 1½ HOURS (+ REFRIGERATION & COOLING) **SERVES** 12

2 SHEETS SHORTCRUST PASTRY
⅔ CUP (160ML) WATER
50G (1½ OUNCES) BUTTER, CHOPPED FINELY
1 TABLESPOON CASTER (SUPERFINE) SUGAR
⅔ CUP (100G) BAKER'S FLOUR
2 EGGS
100G (3 OUNCES) CANDIED ORANGE SLICES, CHOPPED FINELY
⅓ CUP (80G) REDCURRANT JELLY
15 SLICES CANDIED ORANGE (200G), EXTRA

PASTRY CREAM

1⅓ CUPS (330ML) MILK
1 VANILLA BEAN, SPLIT IN HALF LENGTHWAYS
3 EGG YOLKS
⅓ CUP (75G) CASTER (SUPERFINE) SUGAR
2 TABLESPOONS CORNFLOUR (CORNSTARCH)
20G (¾ OUNCE) BUTTER

1 Place oven tray in oven; preheat oven to 220°C/425°F.

2 Join pastry sheets, overlapping about 5mm (¼ inch); brush between overlap with a little tap water, press firmly to seal. Line lightly greased 34cm x 11cm (13½-inch x 4½-inch) rectangular loose-based fluted tart tin with pastry. Trim excess pastry, leaving about 5mm (¼ inch) above edges to account for shrinkage; prick base all over with a fork. Place tin on preheated oven tray. Line pastry with baking paper; fill with dried beans or rice. Bake for 10 minutes. Remove paper and beans; bake for a further 5 minutes. Remove pastry from oven. Reduce oven to 200°C/400°F.

3 Meanwhile, make pastry cream.

4 Combine the water, butter and sugar in a medium saucepan; bring to the boil. Add flour; beat with a wooden spoon over medium heat until mixture comes away from the base of the pan. Transfer choux pastry to a medium bowl; stand 1 minute. Beat in eggs, one at a time, until pastry becomes smooth and glossy.

5 Cover base of tart shell with chopped candied orange.

6 Beat pastry cream and choux pastry in medium bowl with an electric mixer until combined. Spoon mixture into tart shell; smooth surface.

7 Bake tart for 45 minutes or until puffed and light brown (cover with aluminium foil if it starts to over-brown). Stand tart in pan 15 minutes before transferring to a wire rack.

8 Heat jelly in microwave oven until warm; pour over warm tart. Place orange slices on tart. Serve warm.

pastry cream Place milk in a medium saucepan; scrape vanilla seeds into milk, add bean. Bring milk mixture to the boil. Meanwhile, whisk egg yolks, sugar and cornflour in a medium heatproof bowl. Gradually whisk hot milk mixture into egg mixture. Strain mixture back into pan, discard bean; whisk over medium heat until it boils and thickens. Remove from heat; whisk in butter until smooth. Cover surface with plastic wrap.

CYGNE CHANTILLY (CHOUX SWANS)

PREP + COOK TIME 1 HOUR (+ REFRIGERATION & COOLING) **MAKES** 8

⅔ CUP (160ML) WATER
50G (1½ OUNCES) BUTTER, CHOPPED FINELY
1 TABLESPOON CASTER (SUPERFINE) SUGAR
⅔ CUP (100G) BAKER'S FLOUR
3 EGGS
PURE ICING (CONFECTIONERS') SUGAR, FOR DUSTING

CHANTILLY CREAM

1½ CUPS (375ML) THICKENED (HEAVY) CREAM
1 TEASPOON VANILLA EXTRACT
2 TABLESPOONS PURE ICING (CONFECTIONERS') SUGAR

1 Preheat oven to 220°C/425°F. Grease oven trays.
2 Combine the water, butter and sugar in a medium saucepan; bring to the boil. Add flour; beat with a wooden spoon over medium heat until mixture comes away from base of pan. Transfer choux pastry to a medium bowl; stand 1 minute. Beat in two of the eggs, one at a time, until pastry becomes smooth and glossy but still holds its shape.
3 Spoon three-quarters of the pastry into a piping bag fitted with a 1cm (½-inch) plain tube. Pipe eight 4cm x 6cm (1½-inch x 2½-inch) swan bodies, about 5cm (2 inches) apart, on trays (see tips). Spoon remaining pastry into a piping bag fitted with a 5mm (¼-inch) plain tube; pipe eight swan necks, 6.5cm (2¾ inches) high on second tray (see tips). Brush bodies with lightly beaten remaining egg.
4 Bake swan necks 5 minutes; remove from oven. Cool on trays.
5 Bake swan bodies 10 minutes. Reduce oven to 160°C/325°F; bake a further 20 minutes. Turn off oven; cool puffs in oven with door ajar.
6 Make chantilly cream.
7 Using a serrated knife, cut the top third off the swan bodies; cut this piece in half to make wings.
8 Spoon three-quarters of the cream into a piping bag fitted with a 1.5cm (¾-inch) fluted tube; pipe cream into bodies. Arrange wings and neck on bodies.
9 Spoon remaining cream into another piping bag fitted with a 5mm (¼-inch) fluted tube. Pipe cream between wings; dust with sifted icing sugar.

chantilly cream Beat ingredients in a small bowl with an electric mixer until firm peaks form. Refrigerate until required.

tips To pipe the swan's body, place the tube close to the tray and press down to finish the choux with a small point. To pipe the neck, start at the base of the neck and finish at the head. As you finish the head, press down on the tube to make a point, which will be the beak. It's a good idea to make double the number of necks, as it can take a few attempts to get the hang of it. If the neck is too thin, it will burn (when piping, you can pipe over the neck once more to thicken it). Once filled, the choux will soften, so assemble 1-2 hours before eating.

PLUM & ALMOND TURNOVERS

PREP + COOK TIME 1¼ HOURS (+ COOLING) **MAKES** 30

825G (1¾ POUNDS) CANNED WHOLE PLUMS IN NATURAL JUICE
¼ CUP (55G) CASTER (SUPERFINE) SUGAR
3 CARDAMOM PODS, BRUISED
2 TABLESPOONS CORNFLOUR (CORNSTARCH)
1 TABLESPOON WATER
250G (8 OUNCES) MARZIPAN, CHOPPED COARSELY
⅓ CUP (80ML) THICKENED (HEAVY) CREAM
6 SHEETS PUFF PASTRY
1 EGG, BEATEN LIGHTLY
¼ CUP (20G) FLAKED ALMONDS
1 TABLESPOON DEMERARA SUGAR
2 TEASPOONS ICING (CONFECTIONERS') SUGAR

1 Drain plums over a small bowl; reserve ½ cup of juice, discard remainder. Cut plums into quarters; discard seeds.
2 Place plums, reserved juice, caster sugar and cardamom in a medium saucepan; stir over high heat, without boiling, until sugar dissolves. Bring to the boil; boil, uncovered, for 5 minutes or until mixture is thickened slightly. Blend cornflour with the water in a small jug, add to pan; cook, stirring, until mixture boils and thickens. Cool 2 hours. Discard cardamom.
3 Meanwhile, blend or process marzipan and cream until smooth.
4 Preheat oven to 200°C/400°F. Grease oven trays; line with baking paper.
5 Cut 30 x 9cm (3¾-inch) rounds from pastry sheets. Spread rounded teaspoons of marzipan mixture over each pastry round, leaving a 1cm (½-inch) border. Divide plum mixture into centres of pastry rounds. Brush edges with egg; fold rounds in half to enclose filling, pinch edges to seal.
6 Place turnovers on trays about 5cm (2 inches) apart. Brush tops with egg; sprinkle with nuts, then demerara sugar.
7 Bake turnovers about 25 minutes. Cool on trays. Serve warm, dusted with icing sugar.
serving suggestion Serve with ice-cream, custard or cream.

APPLE PIE WITH PASSIONFRUIT ICING

PREP + COOK TIME 1 HOUR 40 MINUTES (+ COOLING) **SERVES** 8

8 MEDIUM APPLES (1.5KG)
⅔ CUP (150G) CASTER (SUPERFINE) SUGAR
½ CUP (125ML) WATER
2 TABLESPOONS WHITE (GRANULATED) SUGAR (OPTIONAL)

PASTRY

3 CUPS (450G) SELF-RAISING FLOUR
¼ CUP (40G) ICING (CONFECTIONERS') SUGAR
125G (4 OUNCES) COLD BUTTER, CHOPPED COARSELY
1 EGG, BEATEN LIGHTLY
½ CUP (125ML) MILK, APPROXIMATELY

PASSIONFRUIT ICING

1½ CUPS (240G) ICING (CONFECTIONERS') SUGAR
2 PASSIONFRUIT

1 Peel, quarter and core apples; slice thickly. Place apples, caster sugar and the water in a large saucepan; cover, bring to the boil. Reduce heat; simmer for 10 minutes or until apples are just tender. Gently spoon the apple mixture into a large colander or strainer to drain. Cool to room temperature.

2 Preheat oven to 200°C/400°F. Grease a 20cm x 30cm (8-inch x 12-inch) lamington pan; line base and long sides with baking paper, extending the paper 5cm (2 inches) over the sides.

3 Make pastry.

4 Roll two-thirds of the pastry on a floured surface until large enough to line base and sides of pan, with 1cm (½ inch) extending over the sides. Lift pastry into pan; ease into base and sides. Spread cold apple mixture into pastry case; brush edges with a little extra milk. Roll out remaining pastry until large enough to generously cover pie. Place over filling; press edges together to seal. Trim excess pastry around edges. Brush top with a little milk; sprinkle with white sugar. Slash about six holes in pastry.

5 Bake pie for 45 minutes. Leave pie in pan for 10 minutes before turning, right-side up, on a wire rack to cool.

6 Meanwhile, make passionfruit icing.

7 Spread icing over pie; serve cut into squares.

pastry Sift flour and icing sugar into a large bowl; rub in butter. Make a well in centre. Using a knife, 'cut' combined egg and enough milk through flour mixture to make a soft dough.

passionfruit icing Sift icing sugar into a medium heatproof bowl; stir in passionfruit pulp, then enough water to make a stiff paste. Place bowl over a medium saucepan of simmering water; stir icing until spreadable.

SPICED APRICOT & PLUM PIE

PREP + COOK TIME 1 HOUR 10 MINUTES (+ COOLING) **SERVES** 8

2 X 825G (1¾ POUNDS) CANNED DARK PLUMS IN LIGHT SYRUP
2 CUPS (300G) DRIED APRICOTS
1 CINNAMON STICK
3 CLOVES
½ TEASPOON MIXED SPICE
½ TEASPOON GROUND GINGER
2 SHEETS PUFF PASTRY
1 EGG, BEATEN LIGHTLY
1 TABLESPOON ICING (CONFECTIONERS') SUGAR

SPICED YOGHURT CREAM

½ CUP (140G) YOGHURT
½ CUP (120G) SOUR CREAM
1 TABLESPOON GROUND CINNAMON
¼ TEASPOON GROUND GINGER

1 Preheat oven to 200°C/400°F. Grease a deep 1.25 litre (5-cup) rectangular baking dish or a 26cm (10½-inch) pie dish.

2 Drain plums; reserve 1 cup of the syrup. Halve plums, discard stones; place plums in dish.

3 Place reserved syrup, apricots, cinnamon, cloves, mixed spice and ginger in a medium saucepan; simmer, uncovered, until liquid is reduced to ½ cup. Remove and discard cinnamon stick and cloves. Cool syrup to room temperature. Pour over plums.

4 Cut pastry into 2.5cm (1-inch) strips. Brush edges of the dish with a little of the egg; press pastry strips around edges of dish. Twist remaining strips, place over filling in a lattice pattern; trim ends, brush top with remaining egg.

5 Bake pie for 40 minutes or until pastry is browned lightly.

6 Make spiced yoghurt cream.

7 Dust pie with icing sugar; serve with spiced yoghurt cream.

spiced yoghurt cream Combine ingredients in a small bowl.

TRADITIONAL APPLE STRUDEL

PREP + COOK TIME 1 HOUR 40 MINUTES (+ STANDING) **SERVES** 6

1.2KG (2½ POUNDS) APPLES
½ CUP (110G) CASTER (SUPERFINE) SUGAR
1 TEASPOON VANILLA EXTRACT
30G (1 OUNCE) BUTTER
1 CUP (70G) STALE BREADCRUMBS
½ CUP (100G) LIGHTLY PACKED BROWN SUGAR
¾ CUP (120G) SULTANAS
1 TEASPOON FINELY GRATED LEMON RIND
1 TEASPOON GROUND CINNAMON
¼ TEASPOON GROUND NUTMEG
185G (6 OUNCES) BUTTER, EXTRA, MELTED
1 TABLESPOON ICING (CONFECTIONERS') SUGAR

PASTRY

1½ CUPS (225G) PLAIN (ALL-PURPOSE) FLOUR
1 EGG
1 TABLESPOON OLIVE OIL
⅓ CUP (80ML) WARM WATER, APPROXIMATELY

1 Peel, core and slice apples thinly. Combine apple slices with caster sugar and extract in a medium bowl. Cover; stand 1 hour.
2 Meanwhile, make pastry.
3 Melt butter in a small frying pan over low heat; stir in breadcrumbs until golden brown. Cool. Combine breadcrumb mixture and brown sugar in a small bowl.
4 Drain excess liquid from apples; return apples to bowl. Add sultanas, rind, cinnamon and nutmeg; stir gently until combined.
5 Preheat oven to 200°C/400°F. Grease a large oven tray.
6 Cover a large table with a clean cloth; rub flour over cloth. Roll out dough as far as it goes. Flour your hands, slip them under the dough; gently and carefully, start lifting and stretching the dough from the centre using the back of your hands, rather than your fingers. Continue stretching the dough until it is paper-thin and approximately 87cm (36 inches) square.
7 Brush pastry with two thirds of the extra melted butter. Sprinkle breadcrumb mixture over half the pastry. Spoon the apple mixture along one end of the pastry, leaving a 5cm (2-inch) border. Fold in the sides of the pastry, cover both ends of the apple filling. Gather the cloth in your hands and carefully roll up the strudel, pulling the cloth toward you as you roll. Place strudel on the tray, gently curving into a horseshoe shape. Brush with remaining melted butter.
8 Bake for 40 minutes or until golden. Cool. Dust with icing sugar.
pastry Sift flour into a medium bowl, make a well in the centre; add egg and oil. Gradually add the water, mixing to a soft dough with your hands. Knead on a floured surface into a ball. Pick up the dough, then throw it down on the floured surface about 100 times. Knead dough for 5 minutes. (The more the dough is banged and kneaded, the lighter it will be.) Form dough into a ball; place in a lightly oiled bowl. Cover; stand in a warm place for 45 minutes.

INDIVIDUAL JAM TARTS

PREP + COOK TIME 45 MINUTES (+ REFRIGERATION) **MAKES** 36

2 CUPS (300G) PLAIN (ALL-PURPOSE) FLOUR
¼ CUP (40G) ICING (CONFECTIONERS') SUGAR
185G (6 OUNCES) COLD UNSALTED BUTTER, CHOPPED COARSELY
1 EGG YOLK
1 TABLESPOON ICED WATER, APPROXIMATELY
⅓ CUP (110G) STRAWBERRY JAM
⅓ CUP (110G) BLACK CHERRY JAM
⅓ CUP (110G) APRICOT JAM
⅓ CUP (110G) RASPBERRY JAM
1 TABLESPOON ICING (CONFECTIONERS') SUGAR, EXTRA

1 Process flour, icing sugar and butter until crumbly. With motor operating, add egg yolk and enough of the water to make ingredients come together. Knead dough on a floured surface until smooth. Divide dough in half; roll one half between sheets of baking paper until 3mm (⅛-inch) thick. Repeat with remaining half. Place on trays; refrigerate 30 minutes.

2 Grease 36 holes of four 12-hole (1-tablespoon/20ml) shallow round-based patty pans.

3 Using a 6cm (2½-inch) round cutter, cut 18 rounds from each piece of pastry; re-roll pastry scraps as necessary. Press pastry rounds into pan holes. Prick pastry cases well with a fork. Refrigerate 30 minutes.

4 Preheat oven to 220°C/425°F.

5 Bake pastry cases about 5 minutes. Using all four jams, drop slightly rounded teaspoons of jam into pastry cases (one type of jam per case).

6 Bake tarts about 10 minutes. Cool. Just before serving, dust with extra icing sugar.

tip You can use just one type of jam for this recipe if you like, but we like using different jams for the variety in colour and taste.

BIG
CAKES

SPONGE ROLL
WITH JAM & CREAM

PREP + COOK TIME 40 MINUTES **SERVES** 8

3 EGGS
⅔ CUP (150G) CASTER (SUPERFINE) SUGAR
½ CUP (75G) WHEATEN CORNFLOUR (CORNSTARCH)
2 TABLESPOONS CUSTARD POWDER
¾ TEASPOON CREAM OF TARTAR
½ TEASPOON BICARBONATE OF SODA (BAKING SODA)
¾ CUP (180ML) THICKENED (HEAVY) CREAM
⅓ CUP (110G) RASPBERRY JAM
1 TABLESPOON ICING (CONFECTIONERS') SUGAR

1 Preheat oven to 180°C/350°F. Grease a 25cm x 30cm (10-inch x 12-inch) swiss roll pan; line base and long sides with baking paper, extending the paper 5cm (2 inches) over the sides.

2 Beat eggs and ½ cup of the caster sugar in a small bowl with an electric mixer until thick and creamy and sugar is dissolved. Fold in triple-sifted dry ingredients.

3 Spread mixture into pan; bake about 12 minutes.

4 Meanwhile, beat cream in a small bowl with an electric mixer until soft peaks form.

5 Place a piece of baking paper cut the same size as pan on the bench; sprinkle with remaining caster sugar. Turn sponge onto paper; peel lining paper away. Cool; trim all sides of sponge.

6 Spread sponge with jam, then cream. Using the paper as a guide, roll the sponge from a short side. Cover with plastic wrap; refrigerate 30 minutes. Before serving, dust with sifted icing sugar.

tips You'll notice most sponge recipes call for triple-sifted flour. We sift the dry ingredients twice onto a piece of greaseproof paper (why create washing up by using a bowl) – this sifting not only mixes the ingredients thoroughly, but also incorporates some air into the flour. Hold the sifter up high as you sift. The third sifting is done over the egg mixture, seconds before you start folding the ingredients together.

HUMMINGBIRD CAKE

PREP + COOK TIME 1¼ HOURS SERVES 12

450G (14½ OUNCES) CANNED CRUSHED PINEAPPLE IN SYRUP
1 CUP (150G) PLAIN (ALL-PURPOSE) FLOUR
½ CUP (75G) SELF-RAISING FLOUR
½ TEASPOON BICARBONATE OF SODA (BAKING SODA)
½ TEASPOON GROUND CINNAMON
½ TEASPOON GROUND GINGER
1 CUP (220G) FIRMLY PACKED BROWN SUGAR
½ CUP (40G) DESICCATED COCONUT
1 CUP MASHED BANANA
2 EGGS, BEATEN LIGHTLY
¾ CUP (180ML) VEGETABLE OIL

PINEAPPLE IN SYRUP

2 TABLESPOONS CASTER (SUPERFINE) SUGAR
½ CUP (125ML) WATER
1 SMALL PINEAPPLE (900G), PEELED, HALVED, SLICED THINLY

CREAM CHEESE FROSTING

60G (2 OUNCES) BUTTER, SOFTENED
120G (4 OUNCES) CREAM CHEESE, SOFTENED
2 TEASPOONS VANILLA EXTRACT
3 CUPS (480G) ICING (CONFECTIONERS') SUGAR

1 Make pineapple in syrup.
2 Preheat oven to 180°C/350°F. Grease a deep 23cm (9-inch) square cake pan; line base with baking paper.
3 Drain pineapple over a medium bowl, pressing with a spoon to extract as much syrup as possible. Reserve ¼ cup of the syrup.
4 Sift flours, soda, spices and sugar into a large bowl. Stir in drained pineapple, reserved syrup, coconut, banana, egg and oil. Pour mixture into pan.
5 Bake cake about 40 minutes. Leave cake in pan for 5 minutes; turn, top-side up, onto a wire rack to cool.
6 Make cream cheese frosting; spread cake with frosting. Top with pineapple slices and a little syrup.

pineapple in syrup Stir sugar and the water in a small saucepan over medium heat, without boiling, until sugar dissolves. Bring to the boil; reduce heat to a simmer (do not stir). Add pineapple, in batches; cook, without stirring, 4 minutes or until softened. Transfer to a plate to cool. Repeat with remaining pineapple. Reserve syrup.

cream cheese frosting Beat butter, cream cheese and extract in a small bowl with an electric mixer until light and fluffy. Gradually beat in sifted icing sugar.

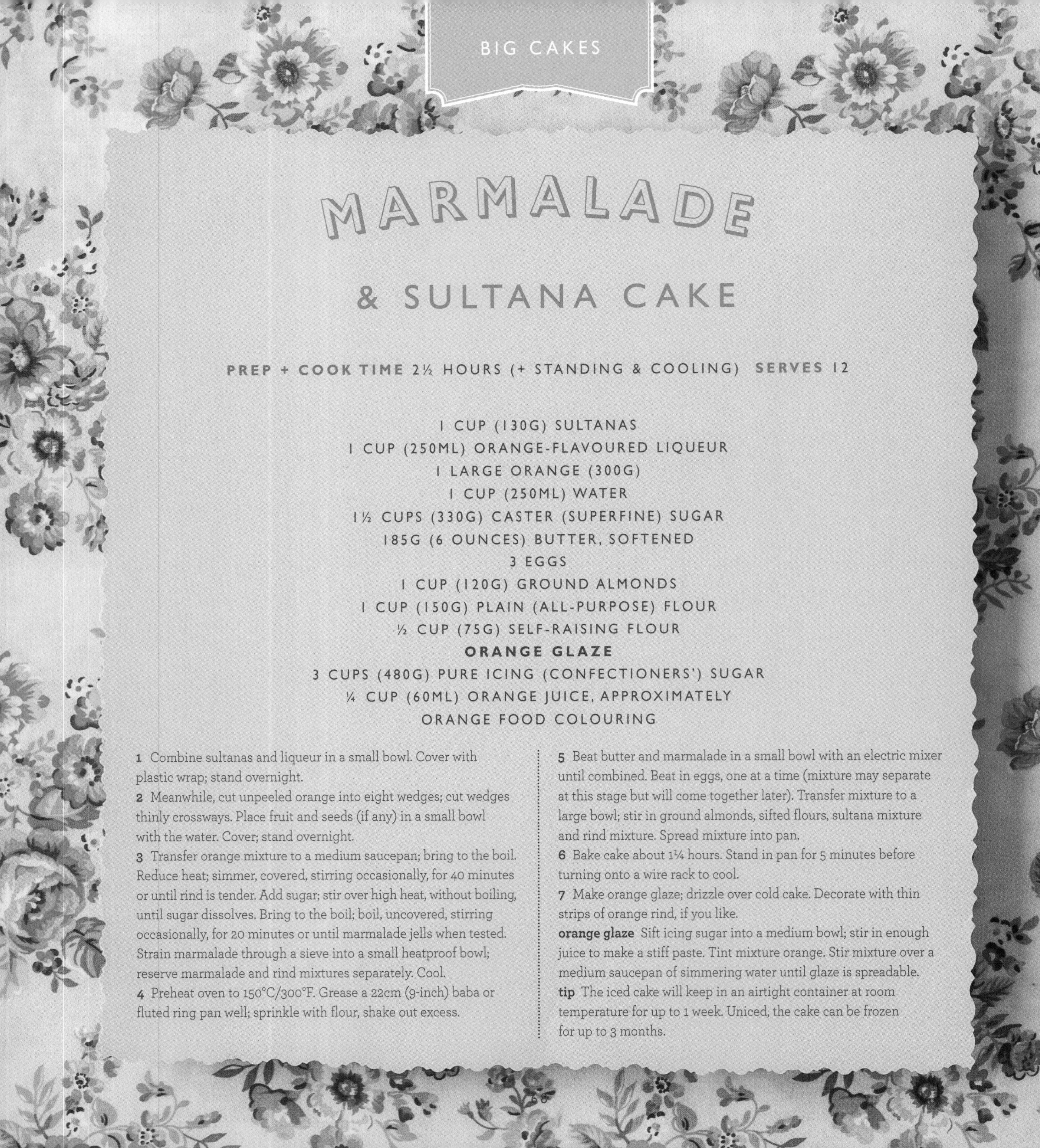

MARMALADE & SULTANA CAKE

PREP + COOK TIME 2½ HOURS (+ STANDING & COOLING) **SERVES** 12

1 CUP (130G) SULTANAS
1 CUP (250ML) ORANGE-FLAVOURED LIQUEUR
1 LARGE ORANGE (300G)
1 CUP (250ML) WATER
1½ CUPS (330G) CASTER (SUPERFINE) SUGAR
185G (6 OUNCES) BUTTER, SOFTENED
3 EGGS
1 CUP (120G) GROUND ALMONDS
1 CUP (150G) PLAIN (ALL-PURPOSE) FLOUR
½ CUP (75G) SELF-RAISING FLOUR

ORANGE GLAZE

3 CUPS (480G) PURE ICING (CONFECTIONERS') SUGAR
¼ CUP (60ML) ORANGE JUICE, APPROXIMATELY
ORANGE FOOD COLOURING

1 Combine sultanas and liqueur in a small bowl. Cover with plastic wrap; stand overnight.

2 Meanwhile, cut unpeeled orange into eight wedges; cut wedges thinly crossways. Place fruit and seeds (if any) in a small bowl with the water. Cover; stand overnight.

3 Transfer orange mixture to a medium saucepan; bring to the boil. Reduce heat; simmer, covered, stirring occasionally, for 40 minutes or until rind is tender. Add sugar; stir over high heat, without boiling, until sugar dissolves. Bring to the boil; boil, uncovered, stirring occasionally, for 20 minutes or until marmalade jells when tested. Strain marmalade through a sieve into a small heatproof bowl; reserve marmalade and rind mixtures separately. Cool.

4 Preheat oven to 150°C/300°F. Grease a 22cm (9-inch) baba or fluted ring pan well; sprinkle with flour, shake out excess.

5 Beat butter and marmalade in a small bowl with an electric mixer until combined. Beat in eggs, one at a time (mixture may separate at this stage but will come together later). Transfer mixture to a large bowl; stir in ground almonds, sifted flours, sultana mixture and rind mixture. Spread mixture into pan.

6 Bake cake about 1¼ hours. Stand in pan for 5 minutes before turning onto a wire rack to cool.

7 Make orange glaze; drizzle over cold cake. Decorate with thin strips of orange rind, if you like.

orange glaze Sift icing sugar into a medium bowl; stir in enough juice to make a stiff paste. Tint mixture orange. Stir mixture over a medium saucepan of simmering water until glaze is spreadable.

tip The iced cake will keep in an airtight container at room temperature for up to 1 week. Uniced, the cake can be frozen for up to 3 months.

CUT-AND-KEEP BUTTER CAKE

PREP + COOK TIME 1½ HOURS **SERVES** 10

125G (4 OUNCES) BUTTER, SOFTENED
1 TEASPOON VANILLA EXTRACT
1¼ CUPS (275G) CASTER (SUPERFINE) SUGAR
3 EGGS
1 CUP (150G) PLAIN (ALL-PURPOSE) FLOUR
½ CUP (75G) SELF-RAISING FLOUR
¼ TEASPOON BICARBONATE OF SODA (BAKING SODA)
½ CUP (125ML) MILK

1 Preheat oven to 180°C/350°F. Grease a deep 20cm (8-inch) round cake pan; line base with baking paper.
2 Beat ingredients in a medium bowl with an electric mixer on low speed until just combined. Increase speed to medium; beat for 3 minutes or until mixture is smooth and pale in colour. Spread mixture into pan.
3 Bake cake about 1¼ hours. Leave cake in pan for 5 minutes before turning, top-side up, onto a wire rack to cool. Serve dusted with sifted icing (confectioners') sugar, if you like.
tip Store butter cake in an airtight container at room temperature for up to 2 days; freeze for up to 2 months.

CLASSIC POUND CAKE

PREP + COOK TIME 1 HOUR 20 MINUTES SERVES 12

250G (8 OUNCES) BUTTER, SOFTENED
1 CUP (220G) CASTER (SUPERFINE) SUGAR
1 TEASPOON VANILLA EXTRACT
4 EGGS
½ CUP (75G) SELF-RAISING FLOUR
1 CUP (150G) PLAIN (ALL-PURPOSE) FLOUR
2 TEASPOONS ICING (CONFECTIONERS') SUGAR

1 Preheat oven to 180°C/350°F. Grease a deep 20cm (8-inch) round cake pan; line base with baking paper.

2 Beat butter, caster sugar and extract in a small bowl with an electric mixer until light and fluffy. Beat in eggs, one at a time. Transfer mixture to a large bowl; fold in sifted flours, in two batches. Spread mixture into pan.

3 Bake cake about 1 hour. Leave cake in pan for 5 minutes before turning, top-side up, onto a wire rack to cool. Serve dusted with sifted icing sugar.

serving suggestion Serve with strawberries and whipped cream.

CARROT CAKE
WITH CREAM CHEESE FROSTING

PREP + COOK TIME 1¾ HOURS (+ COOLING) SERVES 12

3 EGGS
1⅓ CUPS (250G) FIRMLY PACKED BROWN SUGAR
1 CUP (250ML) VEGETABLE OIL
3 CUPS COARSELY GRATED CARROT
1 CUP (120G) COARSELY CHOPPED WALNUTS
2½ CUPS (375G) SELF-RAISING FLOUR
½ TEASPOON BICARBONATE OF SODA (BAKING SODA)
2 TEASPOONS MIXED SPICE
15G (½ OUNCE) BUTTER
2 TEASPOONS BROWN SUGAR, EXTRA
2 TEASPOONS GROUND CINNAMON
1 CUP (100G) ROASTED WALNUTS, EXTRA

CREAM CHEESE FROSTING
65G (2 OUNCES) BUTTER, SOFTENED
165G (4 OUNCES) CREAM CHEESE, SOFTENED
2¼ TEASPOONS FINELY GRATED LEMON RIND
3½ CUPS (540G) ICING (CONFECTIONERS') SUGAR

1 Preheat oven to 180°C/350°F. Grease a deep 22cm (9-inch) round cake pan; line base with baking paper.
2 Beat eggs, sugar and oil in a small bowl with an electric mixer until thick and creamy. Transfer mixture to a large bowl; stir in carrot and walnuts, then sifted dry ingredients. Pour mixture into pan.
3 Bake cake about 1¼ hours. Leave cake in pan for 5 minutes before turning, top-side up, onto a wire rack to cool.
4 Meanwhile, melt butter in a small saucepan over medium heat; stir in extra brown sugar, cinnamon and extra walnuts. Cool.
5 Make cream cheese frosting.
6 Split cold cake in half, place bottom layer onto a serving plate, cut-side up; spread with half the frosting. Top with remaining cake layer; spread top with remaining frosting. Decorate with caramel walnuts.

cream cheese frosting Beat butter, cream cheese and rind in a small bowl with an electric mixer until light and fluffy. Gradually beat in sifted icing sugar.

tips You will need 3 large carrots (540g) for the amount of grated carrot in this recipe. This cake will keep in an airtight container in the fridge for up to 3 days. Without the frosting and walnuts, the cake can be frozen for up to 3 months.

ORANGE POPPY SEED SYRUP CAKE

PREP + COOK TIME 1½ HOURS (+ STANDING) **SERVES** 16

⅓ CUP (50G) POPPY SEEDS
¼ CUP (60ML) MILK
185G (6 OUNCES) BUTTER, SOFTENED
1 TABLESPOON FINELY GRATED ORANGE RIND
1 CUP (220G) CASTER (SUPERFINE) SUGAR
3 EGGS
1½ CUPS (225G) SELF-RAISING FLOUR
½ CUP (75G) PLAIN (ALL-PURPOSE) FLOUR
½ CUP (60G) GROUND ALMONDS
½ CUP (125ML) ORANGE JUICE

ORANGE SYRUP

1 CUP (220G) CASTER (SUPERFINE) SUGAR
⅔ CUP (160ML) ORANGE JUICE
⅓ CUP (80ML) WATER

1 Combine seeds and milk in a small bowl; stand for 20 minutes.

2 Preheat oven to 180°C/350°F. Grease a deep 22cm (9-inch) round cake pan; line base and side with baking paper.

3 Beat butter, rind and sugar in a small bowl with an electric mixer until light and fluffy; beat in eggs, one at a time. Transfer mixture to a large bowl; using a wooden spoon, stir in sifted flours, ground almonds, juice and poppy-seed mixture. Spread mixture into pan; bake about 1 hour.

4 Meanwhile, make orange syrup.

5 Leave cake in pan for 5 minutes before turning, top-side up, onto a wire rack set over a tray. Pour hot syrup over hot cake; serve warm.

orange syrup Using a wooden spoon, stir ingredients in a small saucepan over heat, without boiling, until sugar dissolves. Bring to the boil; reduce heat, simmer, uncovered, without stirring, for 2 minutes.

tips Lemon or mandarin flavours also blend with the taste of poppy seeds; substitute, in equal amounts, for the orange rind and juice given in the recipe. Store the cake, coated with syrup, in an airtight container for up to 2 days. The cake, without syrup, can be stored in an airtight container for up to 2 days, and can also be frozen for up to 3 months.

CHOCOLATE

SPONGE ROLL

PREP + COOK TIME 45 MINUTES (+ COOLING) **SERVES** 10

4 EGGS, SEPARATED
½ CUP (110G) CASTER (SUPERFINE) SUGAR
2 TABLESPOONS HOT WATER
60G (2 OUNCES) DARK (SEMI-SWEET) CHOCOLATE, GRATED COARSELY
½ CUP (75G) SELF-RAISING FLOUR
2 TABLESPOONS CASTER (SUPERFINE) SUGAR, EXTRA
150G (4½ OUNCES) DARK (SEMI-SWEET) CHOCOLATE, EXTRA, MELTED
250G (8 OUNCES) FRESH RASPBERRIES

RASPBERRY VANILLA CREAM

1½ CUPS (375ML) THICKENED (HEAVY) CREAM
1 TABLESPOON ICING (CONFECTIONERS') SUGAR
2 TEASPOONS VANILLA EXTRACT
1 CUP FRESH OR FROZEN RASPBERRIES, PUREED

1 Preheat oven to 180°C/350°F. Grease a 23cm x 32cm (9-inch x 13-inch) swiss roll pan; line base and long sides with baking paper, extending the paper 5cm (2 inches) over the sides.

2 Beat egg yolks and sugar in a small bowl with an electric mixer for about 5 minutes or until thick and creamy. Transfer mixture to a large bowl; fold in the hot water and grated chocolate, then fold in sifted flour.

3 Beat egg whites in a small bowl with the electric mixer until soft peaks form; fold into chocolate mixture. Spread mixture into pan. Bake cake about 12 minutes.

4 Meanwhile, place a piece of baking paper cut the same size as the pan on bench; sprinkle with extra sugar.

5 Turn hot sponge onto the sugared paper; peel away lining paper. Using paper as a guide, loosely roll sponge from long side. Stand for 2 minutes; unroll. Cool; trim all sides of sponge.

6 Make raspberry vanilla cream.

7 Spread sponge with cream. Using paper as a guide, roll sponge up from long side. Drizzle roll with melted chocolate; sprinkle with raspberries. Stand until chocolate sets. Dust with a little icing sugar.

raspberry vanilla cream Beat cream, sifted icing sugar and extract in a small bowl with an electric mixer until soft peaks form. Fold raspberry puree through cream.

tip Filled sponge roll is best eaten the day it is made; store in an airtight container, in the fridge, until ready to serve.

MARBLE CAKE
WITH BUTTER FROSTING

PREP + COOK TIME 1 HOUR 40 MINUTES **SERVES** 12

250G (8 OUNCES) BUTTER, SOFTENED
1 TEASPOON VANILLA EXTRACT
1¼ CUPS (275G) CASTER (SUPERFINE) SUGAR
3 EGGS
2¼ CUPS (335G) SELF-RAISING FLOUR
¾ CUP (180ML) MILK
PINK FOOD COLOURING
2 TABLESPOONS COCOA POWDER
2 TABLESPOONS MILK, EXTRA
BUTTER FROSTING
125G (4 OUNCES) BUTTER, SOFTENED
2 CUPS (320G) ICING (CONFECTIONERS') SUGAR
2 TABLESPOONS MILK

1 Preheat oven to 180°C/350°F. Grease a deep 22cm (9-inch) round cake pan; line base with baking paper.

2 Beat butter, extract and sugar in a medium bowl with an electric mixer until light and fluffy. Beat in eggs, one at a time. Stir in sifted flour and milk, in two batches.

3 Divide mixture into three bowls; tint one mixture pink. Blend sifted cocoa with extra milk in a cup; stir into second mixture. Leave remaining mixture plain. Drop alternate spoonfuls of mixtures into pan. Pull a skewer backwards and forwards through cake mixture to create a marble effect.

4 Bake cake about 1 hour. Leave cake in pan for 5 minutes before turning, top-side up, onto a wire rack to cool.

5 Meanwhile, make butter frosting.

6 Spread frosting all over cold cake.

butter frosting Beat butter in a small bowl with an electric mixer until light and fluffy. Beat in sifted icing sugar and milk, in two batches.

tips The traditional colours for a marble cake are chocolate brown, pink and white, but you can use any food colouring you like. Make the colours fairly strong for maximum impact, as they may fade during baking. This cake will keep in an airtight container at room temperature for up to 3 days. Uniced, the cake can be frozen for up to 3 months.

ECONOMICAL BOILED FRUIT CAKE

PREP + COOK TIME 1¾ HOURS (+ COOLING) **SERVES** 12

2¾ CUPS (500G) MIXED DRIED FRUIT
1 CUP (220G) FIRMLY PACKED BROWN SUGAR
125G (4 OUNCES) BUTTER, CHOPPED
½ CUP (125ML) WATER
1 TEASPOON MIXED SPICE
½ TEASPOON BICARBONATE OF SODA (BAKING SODA)
½ CUP (125ML) SWEET SHERRY
1 EGG
1 CUP (150G) PLAIN (ALL-PURPOSE) FLOUR
1 CUP (150G) SELF-RAISING FLOUR
⅓ CUP (55G) BLANCHED ALMONDS
2 TABLESPOONS SWEET SHERRY, EXTRA

1 Stir fruit, sugar, butter, the water, mixed spice and soda in a large saucepan over low heat, without boiling, until sugar dissolves and butter melts; bring to the boil. Reduce heat; simmer, covered, for 5 minutes. Remove from heat; stir in sherry. Cool to room temperature.
2 Preheat oven to 160°C/325°F. Grease a deep 20cm (8-inch) round cake pan; line base and side with two layers of baking paper, extending the paper 5cm (2 inches) above the side.
3 Stir egg and sifted flours into fruit mixture. Spread mixture into pan; decorate with almonds.
4 Bake cake about 1½ hours. Brush top of hot cake with extra sherry. Cover cake with foil; cool in pan.

tips Cover the cake loosely with foil during baking if it starts to overbrown; and give it quarter turns several times during baking if it is browning unevenly. This cake can be made up to 1 month ahead. Store in an airtight container in a cool, dry place; refrigerate if humid.

FEATHERLIGHT SPONGE

PREP + COOK TIME 40 MINUTES (+ STANDING) **SERVES** 10

4 EGGS
¾ CUP (165G) CASTER (SUPERFINE) SUGAR
⅔ CUP (150G) WHEATEN CORNFLOUR (CORNSTARCH)
¼ CUP (30G) CUSTARD POWDER
1 TEASPOON CREAM OF TARTAR
½ TEASPOON BICARBONATE OF SODA (BAKING SODA)
300ML THICKENED (HEAVY) CREAM
1 TEASPOON VANILLA EXTRACT
¼ CUP (80G) STRAWBERRY JAM
250G (8 OUNCES) STRAWBERRIES, SLICED THINLY
125G (4 OUNCES) STRAWBERRIES, EXTRA, HALVED

ICING

1 CUP (160G) ICING (CONFECTIONERS') SUGAR
10G (½ OUNCE) BUTTER, SOFTENED
1½ TABLESPOONS MILK, APPROXIMATELY

1 Preheat oven to 200°C/400°F. Grease and flour two deep 22cm (9-inch) round cake pans; shake out the excess flour.

2 Beat eggs and sugar in a small bowl with an electric mixer for 7 minutes, until thick and creamy (see tips). Transfer mixture to a large bowl.

3 Sift dry ingredients twice onto a piece of baking paper. Sift flour mixture a third time evenly onto egg mixture. Using a balloon whisk or large metal spoon, quickly and lightly fold flour mixture through egg mixture until incorporated. Pour evenly into pans; tilt pans to spread mixture to the edge.

4 Bake sponges for 20 minutes or until they spring back when pressed lightly in the centre. Turn sponges immediately, top-side up, onto baking-paper-covered wire racks. Cool.

5 Beat cream and extract in a small bowl with an electric mixer until firm peaks form.

6 Place one sponge on a cake stand or plate, spread with jam and cream; top with sliced strawberries.

7 Make icing.

8 Turn remaining sponge top-side down on wire rack; spread with warm icing. Place icing-topped sponge on other sponge. Stand for 15 minutes or until icing is set. Top with extra strawberries; dust with a little icing sugar, if you like.

icing Sift icing sugar into a medium heatproof bowl; stir in butter and enough milk to form a firm paste. (Add the milk gradually, as just a small amount can alter the consistency.) Place the bowl over a medium saucepan of simmering water; stir until icing is a pouring consistency.

tips Using a small bowl when beating the eggs and sugar in step 2 will maximise volume. To test when the mixture is thick and creamy, turn off mixer then lift the beaters – the mixture should form thick ribbons. Before baking, tap the sponge on the base of the pan with your fingers to remove large air pockets. This recipe is best made on the day of serving. The sponge can be filled several hours before.

COFFEE & WALNUT CAKE WITH TOFFEE

PREP + COOK TIME 1¼ HOURS (+ COOLING & STANDING) **SERVES** 8

30G (1 OUNCE) BUTTER
1 TABLESPOON BROWN SUGAR
2 TEASPOONS GROUND CINNAMON
2 CUPS (200G) ROASTED WALNUTS
½ CUP (125ML) MILK
1 TABLESPOON INSTANT COFFEE GRANULES
185G (6 OUNCES) BUTTER, SOFTENED, EXTRA
1⅓ CUPS (300G) CASTER (SUPERFINE) SUGAR
3 EGGS
1 CUP (150G) SELF-RAISING FLOUR
¾ CUP (110G) PLAIN (ALL-PURPOSE) FLOUR

TOFFEE

½ CUP (110G) CASTER (SUPERFINE) SUGAR
2 TABLESPOONS WATER
3 TEASPOONS POURING CREAM

1 Preheat oven to 160°C/325°F. Grease a 22cm (9-inch) baba cake pan well; dust with flour, shake out excess.

2 Melt butter in a small saucepan over medium heat; stir in brown sugar, cinnamon and walnuts. Cool.

3 Combine milk and coffee in a small bowl; stir until coffee dissolves.

4 Beat extra butter and caster sugar in a small bowl with an electric mixer until light and fluffy. Beat in eggs, one at a time. Stir in sifted flours, then milk mixture.

5 Spread one-third of the cake mixture into the pan; sprinkle with half the nut mixture. Top with remaining cake mixture.

6 Bake cake about 45 minutes. Leave cake in pan for 5 minutes before turning onto a wire rack over an oven tray. Cool.

7 Make toffee. Working quickly, drizzle some of the toffee over top of cake, press on remaining nut mixture; drizzle with remaining toffee.

toffee Stir sugar and the water in a small saucepan over medium heat, without boiling, until sugar dissolves; bring to the boil. Reduce heat; simmer, uncovered, without stirring, until toffee becomes caramel in colour. Add cream; stir for 1 minute or until thickened slightly.

tip This cake is best eaten the day it is made.

CINNAMON TEACAKE

PREP + COOK TIME 50 MINUTES **SERVES** 8

60G (2 OUNCES) BUTTER, SOFTENED
⅔ CUP (150G) CASTER (SUPERFINE) SUGAR
1 TEASPOON VANILLA EXTRACT
1 EGG
1 CUP (150G) SELF-RAISING FLOUR
⅓ CUP (80ML) MILK
10G (½ OUNCE) BUTTER, MELTED
1 TEASPOON GROUND CINNAMON
1 TABLESPOON CASTER (SUPERFINE) SUGAR, EXTRA

1 Preheat oven to 180°C/350°F. Grease a deep 20cm (8-inch) round cake pan; line base with baking paper.
2 Beat butter, sugar, extract and egg in a small bowl with an electric mixer until light and fluffy. Stir in sifted flour and milk until smooth. Spread mixture into pan.
3 Bake cake about 30 minutes. Turn cake, top-side up, onto a wire rack. Brush top of hot cake with melted butter; sprinkle with combined cinnamon and extra sugar while hot.
serving suggestion Serve warm with butter.

BLACK FOREST LAYER CAKE

PREP + COOK TIME 2¼ HOURS (+ COOLING) **SERVES** 12

250G (8 OUNCES) BUTTER, CHOPPED
1 TABLESPOON INSTANT COFFEE GRANULES
1½ CUPS (375ML) HOT WATER
200G (6½ OUNCES) DARK (SEMI-SWEET) CHOCOLATE, CHOPPED
2 CUPS (440G) CASTER (SUPERFINE) SUGAR
1½ CUPS (225G) SELF-RAISING FLOUR
1 CUP (150G) PLAIN (ALL-PURPOSE) FLOUR
¼ CUP (25G) COCOA POWDER
2 EGGS
2 TEASPOONS VANILLA EXTRACT
600ML THICKENED (HEAVY) CREAM
¼ CUP (60ML) CHERRY-FLAVOURED LIQUEUR
850G (1¾ POUNDS) CANNED STONELESS BLACK CHERRIES, DRAINED, HALVED
DARK (SEMI-SWEET) CHOCOLATE, EXTRA, SHAVED, TO DECORATE
MARASCHINO CHERRIES, TO DECORATE

1 Preheat oven to 150°C/300°F. Grease a deep 23cm (9-inch) round cake pan; line base and side with baking paper.

2 Melt butter in a medium saucepan over low heat, add combined coffee and hot water, then chocolate and sugar; stir, over low heat, without boiling, until smooth. Transfer to a large bowl of an electric mixer; cool until warm.

3 Beat mixture on low speed with electric mixer; gradually beat in sifted dry ingredients, in three batches. Beat in eggs, one at a time, then extract. Pour mixture into pan.

4 Bake cake about 1¾ hours. Leave cake in pan for 5 minutes before turning, top-side up, onto a wire rack to cool.

5 Beat cream in a small bowl with the electric mixer until firm peaks form.

6 Level top of cake. Split cake into three even layers. Place one cake layer on a serving plate, brush with 1 tablespoon of the liqueur; top with one-third of the cream and half the black cherries. Repeat layering, finishing with a cake layer. Brush top of cake with remaining liqueur; top with remaining cream. Decorate with chocolate shavings and maraschino cherries. Just before serving, dust with a little cocoa powder, if you like.

LUMBERJACK CAKE

PREP + COOK TIME 1¾ HOURS **SERVES** 12

2 LARGE APPLES (400G), PEELED, CORED, CHOPPED FINELY
1 CUP (150G) FINELY CHOPPED SEEDED DRIED DATES
1 TEASPOON BICARBONATE OF SODA (BAKING SODA)
1 CUP (250ML) BOILING WATER
125G (4 OUNCES) BUTTER, SOFTENED
1 TEASPOON VANILLA EXTRACT
1 CUP (220G) CASTER (SUPERFINE) SUGAR
1 EGG
1½ CUPS (225G) PLAIN (ALL-PURPOSE) FLOUR
FLAKED FRESH COCONUT, TO DECORATE (OPTIONAL)

COCONUT TOPPING

60G (2 OUNCES) BUTTER, CHOPPED
½ CUP (110G) FIRMLY PACKED BROWN SUGAR
½ CUP (125ML) MILK
⅔ CUP (50G) SHREDDED COCONUT

1 Preheat oven to 180°C/350°F. Grease a deep 23cm (9-inch) square cake pan; line base and sides with baking paper.
2 Place apple, dates and soda in a large bowl, stir in the water. Cover with plastic wrap; stand 10 minutes.
3 Meanwhile, beat butter, extract, sugar and egg in a small bowl with an electric mixer until light and fluffy. Add butter mixture to apple mixture; stir to combine. Stir in sifted flour until combined.
4 Pour cake mixture into pan; bake about 50 minutes.
5 Meanwhile, make coconut topping.
6 Remove cake from oven; using a metal spatula, carefully spread warm coconut topping evenly over cake. Return to oven; bake for a further 20 minutes or until topping is browned. Leave cake in pan for 5 minutes before turning, top-side up, onto a wire rack to cool. Just before serving, sprinkle with flaked coconut.

coconut topping Stir ingredients in a medium saucepan over low heat until butter melts and sugar dissolves.

tip Cake can be made 3 days ahead; store in an airtight container. Cake can be frozen for up to 3 months.

DARK
GINGERBREAD CAKE

PREP + COOK TIME 1 HOUR **SERVES** 14

125G (4 OUNCES) BUTTER, SOFTENED
½ CUP (110G) FIRMLY PACKED DARK BROWN SUGAR
2 EGGS
1⅔ CUPS (250G) PLAIN (ALL-PURPOSE) FLOUR
½ TEASPOON BICARBONATE OF SODA (BAKING SODA)
2 TEASPOONS GROUND GINGER
1 CUP (360G) TREACLE
2 TABLESPOONS MILK
¼ CUP (55G) FINELY CHOPPED GLACÉ GINGER
⅓ CUP (55G) FINELY CHOPPED RAISINS
STRIPS OF LEMON RIND AND SLICED CRYSTALLISED GINGER, TO DECORATE

LEMON GLACÉ ICING

2 CUPS (320G) ICING (CONFECTIONERS') SUGAR
20G (¾ OUNCE) BUTTER, SOFTENED
2 TABLESPOONS LEMON JUICE

1 Preheat oven to 180°C/350°F. Grease a 20cm x 30cm (8-inch x 12-inch) rectangular cake pan; line base and sides with baking paper, extending the paper 5cm (2 inches) above sides.

2 Beat butter and sugar in a small bowl with an electric mixer until light and fluffy. Beat in eggs, one at a time. Transfer mixture to a large bowl; stir in sifted flour, soda and ground ginger, treacle, milk, glacé ginger and raisins. Spread mixture into pan.

3 Bake cake for 45 minutes or until a skewer inserted into the centre comes out clean. Leave cake in pan for 5 minutes before turning, top-side up, onto a wire rack to cool.

4 Meanwhile, make lemon glacé icing.

5 Spread cold cake with icing; stand until icing is set. Sprinkle with strips of rind and crystallised ginger before cutting.

lemon glacé icing Sift icing sugar into a medium bowl. Stir in butter and juice until icing is smooth and spreadable.

tip Iced cake will keep in an airtight container for up to 3 days. Uniced cake can be frozen for up to 3 months.

APRICOT CHOC CHIP CAKE

PREP + COOK TIME 1¾ HOURS **SERVES** 10

1 CUP (150G) CHOPPED DRIED APRICOTS
1 CUP (250ML) APRICOT NECTAR
125G (4 OUNCES) BUTTER, SOFTENED
⅔ CUP (150G) RAW SUGAR
2 EGGS, SEPARATED
1½ CUPS (120G) DESICCATED COCONUT
1½ CUPS (225G) SELF-RAISING FLOUR
½ CUP (95G) CHOC BITS
1 TABLESPOON ICING (CONFECTIONERS') SUGAR

1 Combine apricots and nectar in a small bowl; stand 1 hour.
2 Preheat oven to 180°C/350°F. Grease a deep 20cm (8-inch) round cake pan; line base with baking paper.
3 Beat butter and sugar in a small bowl with an electric mixer until light and fluffy. Beat in eggs yolks, one at a time, until combined. Transfer mixture to a large bowl; stir in coconut, then half the sifted flour and half the apricot mixture. Stir in remaining flour and apricots, then Choc Bits.
4 Beat egg whites in a small bowl until soft peaks form; fold into cake mixture. Spread mixture into pan.
5 Bake cake about 1¼ hours. Leave cake in pan for 5 minutes before turning onto a wire rack to cool. Dust with sifted icing sugar before serving.
tip This cake will keep in an airtight container for up to 3 days.

APPLE CAKE
WITH APRICOT GLAZE

PREP + COOK TIME 1¾ HOURS **SERVES** 8

185G (6 OUNCES) BUTTER, SOFTENED
2 TEASPOONS GRATED LEMON RIND
⅔ CUP (150G) CASTER (SUPERFINE) SUGAR
3 EGGS
1 CUP (150G) SELF-RAISING FLOUR
½ CUP (75G) PLAIN (ALL-PURPOSE) FLOUR
⅓ CUP (80ML) MILK
2 MEDIUM APPLES (300G)
1 TEASPOON GELATINE
2 TABLESPOONS WATER
2 TABLESPOONS APRICOT JAM, SIEVED

1 Preheat oven to 180°C/350°F. Grease a 20cm (8-inch) springform pan.

2 Beat butter, rind and sugar in a small bowl with an electric mixer until light and fluffy. Beat in eggs, one at a time, until combined. Transfer mixture to a large bowl; stir in sifted flours and milk. Spread mixture into pan.

3 Peel apples; cut into quarters, remove cores. Make lengthways cuts into rounded sides of apple quarters, cutting about three quarters of the way through. Arrange quarters, rounded side up, around edge of cake mixture.

4 Bake cake for 1 hour or until a skewer is inserted into the centre comes out clean.

5 Sprinkle gelatine over the water in a small heatproof jug, stand jug in a small saucepan of simmering water; stir until gelatine dissolves. Stir in jam.

6 Spread half the jam mixture over hot cake; cool cake in pan. Remove cake from pan, brush with remaining warmed jam mixture.

tip This cake will keep in an airtight container at room temperature for up to 2 days.

MANGO COCONUT CAKE

PREP + COOK TIME 1¾ HOURS SERVES 12

250G (8 OUNCES) BUTTER, SOFTENED
1 TEASPOON COCONUT ESSENCE
1½ CUPS (330G) CASTER (SUPERFINE) SUGAR
4 EGGS
⅔ CUP (160ML) MANGO PUREE
2 CUPS (180G) DESICCATED COCONUT
2½ CUPS (375G) SELF-RAISING FLOUR
SHREDDED COCONUT, TO DECORATE

COCONUT FROSTING

1 EGG WHITE
1¼ CUPS (200G) ICING (CONFECTIONERS') SUGAR
2 TEASPOONS MANGO PUREE
¾ CUP (65G) DESICCATED COCONUT
½ CUP (125G) MASCARPONE CHEESE

1 Preheat oven to 180°C/350°F. Grease a deep 22cm (9-inch) round cake pan; line base with baking paper.

2 Beat butter, essence and sugar in a small bowl with an electric mixer until combined. Add eggs, one at a time, beating only until combined between additions. Transfer mixture to a large bowl. Using a wooden spoon, stir in puree and desiccated coconut, then sifted flour. Spread mixture into pan.

3 Bake cake about 1¼ hours. Leave cake in pan for 5 minutes before turning, top-side up, onto a wire rack to cool.

4 Meanwhile, make coconut frosting.

5 Spread cold cake with frosting. Just before serving, sprinkle with shredded coconut.

coconut frosting Beat egg white in a small bowl with an electric mixer until foamy. Gradually beat in sifted icing sugar, 1 tablespoon at a time. Using a fork, mix in puree, coconut and mascarpone. Cover frosting with plastic wrap until required, pressing plastic directly onto surface to stop it drying out.

RASPBERRY CREAM SPONGE

PREP + COOK TIME 50 MINUTES (+ COOLING) **SERVES** 16

4 EGGS
¾ CUP (165G) CASTER (SUPERFINE) SUGAR
⅔ CUP (100G) WHEATEN CORNFLOUR (CORNSTARCH)
¼ CUP (30G) CUSTARD POWDER
1 TEASPOON CREAM OF TARTAR
½ TEASPOON BICARBONATE OF SODA (BAKING SODA)
1½ CUPS (375ML) THICKENED (HEAVY) CREAM
¾ CUP (240G) RASPBERRY JAM

RASPBERRY GLACÉ ICING

45G (1½ OUNCES) FRESH RASPBERRIES
2 CUPS (320G) ICING (CONFECTIONERS') SUGAR
15G (½ OUNCE) BUTTER, SOFTENED
2 TEASPOONS HOT WATER, APPROXIMATELY

1 Preheat oven to 180°C/350°F. Grease a deep 22cm (9-inch) square cake pan.

2 Beat eggs and sugar in a small bowl with an electric mixer for 10 minutes or until thick and creamy and sugar has dissolved; transfer to a large bowl. Sift dry ingredients twice, then sift a third time over egg mixture; fold dry ingredients into egg mixture. Spread mixture into pan.

3 Bake sponge about 25 minutes. Turn sponge immediately onto a baking-paper-covered wire rack, then turn top-side up to cool.

4 Meanwhile, beat cream in a small bowl with an electric mixer until firm peaks form.

5 Make raspberry glacé icing.

6 Split sponge in half. Sandwich with jam and whipped cream. Spread top of sponge with icing; top with extra fresh raspberries, if you like.

raspberry glacé icing Push raspberries through a fine sieve into a small heatproof bowl; discard solids. Sift icing sugar into same bowl; stir in butter and enough of the water to make a thick paste. Place bowl over a small saucepan of simmering water; stir until icing is spreadable.

tip Use a serrated or electric knife to split the sponge.

PECAN SOUR CREAM CAKE

PREP + COOK TIME 1½ HOURS **SERVES** 12

250G (8 OUNCES) BUTTER, SOFTENED
1 TEASPOON VANILLA EXTRACT
¾ CUP (165G) CASTER (SUPERFINE) SUGAR
2 EGGS
300G (9½ OUNCES) SOUR CREAM
1½ CUPS (225G) PLAIN (ALL-PURPOSE) FLOUR
½ CUP (75G) SELF-RAISING FLOUR
1 TEASPOON BICARBONATE OF SODA (BAKING SODA)
½ CUP (60G) FINELY CHOPPED PECANS
2 TABLESPOONS BROWN SUGAR
½ TEASPOON GROUND CINNAMON

1 Preheat oven to 180°C/350°F. Grease a deep 23cm (9-inch) round cake pan; line base with baking paper.
2 Beat butter, extract and sugar in a small bowl with an electric mixer until light and fluffy. Beat in eggs, one at a time. Transfer mixture to a large bowl; stir in sour cream, then sifted flours and soda.
3 Combine pecans, brown sugar and cinnamon in a small bowl.
4 Spread half the cake mixture over base of pan; sprinkle evenly with half the pecan mixture. Spread remaining cake mixture on top; sprinkle with remaining pecan mixture, pressing gently into the cake mixture.
5 Bake cake about 1 hour. Leave cake in pan for 5 minutes before turning, top-side up, onto a wire rack to cool.

CHOC-STRAWBERRY MERINGUE GATEAU

PREP + COOK TIME 1½ HOURS **SERVES** 12

125G (4 OUNCES) BUTTER, SOFTENED
4 EGGS, SEPARATED
¾ CUP (165G) CASTER (SUPERFINE) SUGAR
1 CUP (150G) SELF-RAISING FLOUR
⅓ CUP (35G) COCOA POWDER
½ TEASPOON BICARBONATE OF SODA (BAKING SODA)
1 CUP (250ML) BUTTERMILK
⅓ CUP (150G) CASTER (SUPERFINE) SUGAR, EXTRA
¼ CUP (30G) COARSELY CHOPPED ROASTED HAZELNUTS
⅔ CUP (160ML) THICKENED (HEAVY) CREAM
1 TABLESPOON ICING (CONFECTIONERS') SUGAR
250G (8 OUNCES) STRAWBERRIES, HALVED

1 Preheat oven to 160°C/325°F. Grease two 20cm (8-inch) round cake pans; line bases and sides with baking paper.
2 Beat butter, egg yolks and caster sugar in a medium bowl with an electric mixer until light and fluffy. Stir in combined sifted flour, cocoa and soda, then buttermilk. Divide mixture between pans.
3 Beat egg whites in a small bowl with the electric mixer until soft peaks form; gradually add extra caster sugar, a tablespoon at a time, beating until sugar dissolves between additions.
4 Divide meringue mixture over cake mixture in pans; using a spatula, spread meringue so cake mixture is completely covered. Sprinkle nuts over meringue mixture on one of the cakes.
5 Bake cakes for 25 minutes. Cover pans loosely with foil; bake for a further 20 minutes. Leave cakes in pans for 5 minutes before turning, top-side up, onto wire racks to cool.
6 Beat cream and icing sugar in a small bowl with the electric mixer until soft peaks form. Place cake without nuts on serving plate; spread with cream mixture. Top with strawberries, then remaining cake.
tip This recipe is best made on the day of serving.

CARAMEL
BUTTER CAKE

PREP + COOK TIME 1¼ HOURS **SERVES** 10

125G (4 OUNCES) BUTTER, SOFTENED
1 CUP (220G) FIRMLY PACKED BROWN SUGAR
1 TEASPOON VANILLA EXTRACT
2 EGGS
1 TABLESPOON GOLDEN SYRUP OR TREACLE
1 CUP (150G) PLAIN (ALL-PURPOSE) FLOUR
½ CUP (75G) SELF-RAISING FLOUR
1 TEASPOON GROUND CINNAMON
½ CUP (125ML) MILK

CARAMEL ICING
1½ CUPS (330G) FIRMLY PACKED BROWN SUGAR
90G (3 OUNCES) BUTTER
2½ TABLESPOONS MILK
1¼ CUPS (200G) ICING (CONFECTIONERS') SUGAR
2 TEASPOONS MILK, EXTRA

1 Preheat oven to 180°C/350°F. Grease a deep 20cm (8-inch) round cake pan; line base with baking paper.
2 Beat butter, sugar and extract in a small bowl with an electric mixer until light and fluffy. Beat in eggs and golden syrup. Stir in sifted flours and cinnamon, and milk in two batches. Spread mixture into pan.
3 Bake cake for 50 minutes or until a skewer inserted into the centre comes out clean. Leave cake in pan for 5 minutes before turning, top-side up, onto a wire rack to cool.
4 Make caramel icing. Spread icing on cold cake before serving.

caramel icing Heat brown sugar, butter and milk in a small saucepan, stirring constantly, over medium heat, without boiling until sugar dissolves. Bring to the boil. Reduce heat; simmer, uncovered, 3 minutes without stirring. Remove from heat; stir in sifted icing sugar. Stir in extra milk until icing is of a spreadable consistency.

tip This cake will keep in an airtight container for up to 3 days. Uniced cake can be frozen for up to 3 months.

BLUEBERRY CAKE WITH VANILLA SYRUP

PREP + COOK TIME 1¼ HOURS **SERVES** 8

125G (4 OUNCES) BUTTER, SOFTENED
½ CUP (110G) CASTER (SUPERFINE) SUGAR
2 EGGS
1¾ CUPS (260G) SELF-RAISING FLOUR
½ CUP (125ML) BUTTERMILK
¾ CUP (110G) FROZEN BLUEBERRIES (SEE TIP)

VANILLA SYRUP

½ CUP (110G) CASTER (SUPERFINE) SUGAR
½ CUP (125ML) WATER
2 TEASPOONS VANILLA EXTRACT

1 Preheat oven to 180°C/350°F. Grease a deep 20cm (8-inch) ring pan; line base and side with baking paper.

2 Beat butter and sugar in a small bowl with an electric mixer until light and fluffy. Beat in eggs, one at a time. Stir in flour and buttermilk, in two batches. Spread mixture into pan. Sprinkle with frozen berries, gently pressing into cake mixture.

3 Bake cake for about 45 minutes. Leave cake in pan for 5 minutes before turning, top-side up, onto a wire rack over a tray.

4 Meanwhile, make vanilla syrup.

5 Drizzle hot syrup over hot cake.

vanilla syrup Stir sugar and water in a small saucepan over medium heat, without boiling, until sugar dissolves. Simmer, uncovered, without stirring, for 2 minutes. Stir in extract.

tip Don't thaw the frozen blueberries before using as they will bleed colour into the cake batter.

VICTORIA SPONGE SANDWICH

PREP + COOK TIME 50 MINUTES **SERVES** 10

250G (8 OUNCES) BUTTER
1 TEASPOON VANILLA EXTRACT
1 CUP (220G) CASTER (SUPERFINE) SUGAR
4 EGGS
⅓ CUP (80ML) MILK
2 CUPS (300G) SELF-RAISING FLOUR
⅓ CUP (110G) RASPBERRY JAM, WARMED
2 TEASPOONS ICING (CONFECTIONERS') SUGAR

1 Preheat oven to 180°C/350°F. Grease two deep 20cm (8-inch) round cake pans; line bases with baking paper.
2 Beat butter, extract and sugar in a small bowl with an electric mixer until light and fluffy. Beat in eggs, one at a time; beat in milk. Transfer mixture to a large bowl. Stir in sifted flour, in two batches, until smooth. Divide mixture between pans.
3 Bake cakes about 30 minutes. Turn cakes, top-side up, onto baking paper-covered wire racks to cool.
4 Sandwich cakes with jam. Serve sponge dusted with sifted icing sugar.

tips This recipe is buttery and light all at the same time. Make sure you beat the butter, sugar and egg mixture thoroughly. For other cake filling ideas, see pages 116 & 117.

BLUEBERRY JAM

SANDWICH VICTORIA SPONGE CAKES FROM PAGE 115 WITH ⅓ CUP BLUEBERRY JAM AND ¾ CUP WHIPPED THICKENED (HEAVY) CREAM. SERVE SPONGE DUSTED WITH SIFTED ICING (CONFECTIONERS') SUGAR.

LEMON BUTTER

SANDWICH VICTORIA SPONGE CAKES FROM PAGE 115 WITH ⅓ CUP LEMON BUTTER AND ¾ CUP WHIPPED THICKENED (HEAVY) CREAM. SERVE SPONGE DUSTED WITH SIFTED ICING (CONFECTIONERS') SUGAR.

Cake FILLINGS

RASPBERYY CREAM

SANDWICH VICTORIA SPONGE CAKES FROM PAGE 115 WITH 125G (4 OUNCES) CHOPPED FRESH RASPBERRIES FOLDED THROUGH ¾ CUP WHIPPED THICKENED (HEAVY) CREAM. SERVE SPONGE DUSTED WITH SIFTED ICING (CONFECTIONERS') SUGAR.

PASSIONFRUIT CREAM

SANDWICH VICTORIA SPONGE CAKES FROM PAGE 115 WITH ¾ CUP WHIPPED THICKENED (HEAVY) CREAM AND THE PULP FROM 2 PASSIONFRUIT. SERVE SPONGE DUSTED WITH SIFTED ICING (CONFECTIONERS') SUGAR.

RHUBARB & PEAR CUSTARD CAKE

PREP + COOK TIME 1½ HOURS **SERVES** 10

125G (4 OUNCES) BUTTER, SOFTENED
¾ CUP (165G) CASTER (SUPERFINE) SUGAR
2 EGGS
1½ CUPS (225G) SELF-RAISING FLOUR
½ CUP (60G) GROUND ALMONDS
2 TABLESPOONS CUSTARD POWDER
½ CUP (125ML) MILK
3 TRIMMED STALKS RHUBARB (250G), CUT INTO 2CM (¾-INCH) PIECES
1 LARGE PEAR (330G), PEELED, SLICED THINLY
½ CUP (160G) APRICOT JAM

CUSTARD

2 TABLESPOONS CUSTARD POWDER
2 TABLESPOONS CASTER (SUPERFINE) SUGAR
1 CUP (250ML) MILK
1 TEASPOON VANILLA EXTRACT
20G (¾ OUNCE) BUTTER

1 Preheat oven to 180°C/350°F. Grease a deep 22cm (9-inch) round cake pan; line base and side with baking paper.

2 Make custard.

3 Beat butter and sugar in a medium bowl with an electric mixer until light and fluffy. Beat in eggs, one at a time. Stir in sifted flour, ground almonds, custard powder and milk.

4 Spoon half the cake mixture into pan; top with half the rhubarb and half the pear. Spread cooled custard over fruit; spread remaining cake mixture over custard. Top with remaining rhubarb and remaining pear. Bake about 1 hour.

5 Place jam in a small saucepan over low heat; heat jam, stirring, until warmed through. Strain.

6 Leave cake in pan for 5 minutes before turning, top-side up, onto a wire rack; brush top with warm jam. Cool.

custard Combine custard powder and sugar in a small saucepan over medium heat; gradually stir in milk. Stir over heat until mixture boils and thickens. Remove from heat, add extract and butter; stir until butter melts. Cover surface of custard completely with plastic wrap to prevent a skin forming; cool to room temperature (do not refrigerate as mixture will not be spreadable).

tips Large firm strawberries can be sliced lengthways and substituted for the rhubarb; apple or nashi can be substituted for the pear; or a combination of any of these fruits (including the rhubarb) can be used. This cake will keep for 1 day in an airtight container in the fridge.

CUPCAKES & KISSES

RASPBERRY & WHITE CHOCOLATE CUPCAKES

PREP + COOK TIME 1½ HOURS (+ COOLING & REFRIGERATION) **MAKES** 12

½ CUP (75G) FRESH RASPBERRIES
1 VANILLA BEAN, HALVED LENGTHWAYS
125G (4 OUNCES) BUTTER, SOFTENED
¾ CUP (165G) CASTER (SUPERFINE) SUGAR
2 EGGS
1½ CUPS (225G) SELF-RAISING FLOUR
½ CUP (125ML) MILK
12 FRESH RASPBERRIES, EXTRA

FLUFFY FROSTING

1 CUP (220G) CASTER (SUPERFINE) SUGAR
¾ CUP (80ML) WATER
3 EGG WHITES
¼ CUP (60G) PUREED RASPBERRIES

1 Preheat oven to 180°C/350°F. Line a 12-hole (⅓-cup/80ml) muffin pan with paper cases.

2 Blend or process raspberries until smooth.

3 Scrape seeds from vanilla bean. Beat butter, sugar and seeds in a small bowl with an electric mixer until light and fluffy. Beat in eggs, one at a time.

4 Transfer mixture to a large bowl. Stir in sifted flour and milk, in two batches. Lightly fold and swirl raspberry puree through mixture. Drop ¼-cups of mixture into paper cases.

5 Bake cupcakes about 25 minutes. Leave cupcakes in pan for 5 minutes before turning top-side up, onto a wire rack to cool.

6 Meanwhile, make fluffy frosting. Pipe the frosting onto the cakes; top with extra raspberries.

fluffy frosting Stir sugar and the water in a small pan over high heat, without boiling, until sugar is dissolved. Boil, uncovered, without stirring, 5 minutes or until syrup reaches 114°C/240°F on a sugar thermometer. Remove from heat, allow bubbles to subside. Towards the end of syrup's cooking time, begin to beat egg whites in a small bowl with an electric mixer on medium speed. Keep beating egg whites while syrup reaches the correct temperature or the egg whites will deflate. With the mixer on medium speed, slowly pour in hot syrup in a thin, steady stream; if the syrup is added too quickly, the frosting won't thicken. Once all the syrup is added, continue beating on medium to high for 10 minutes or until the mixture is thick and stands in stiff peaks; the frosting should be barely warm at this stage. Swirl pureed berries through frosting. Use at once.

SPICY BANANA KISSES

PREP + COOK TIME 45 MINUTES **MAKES** 20

125G (4 OUNCES) BUTTER, SOFTENED
½ CUP (110G) FIRMLY PACKED BROWN SUGAR
1 EGG
⅓ CUP MASHED BANANA
⅔ CUP (160ML) BUTTERMILK
1¼ CUPS (185G) PLAIN (ALL-PURPOSE) FLOUR
¼ CUP (35G) SELF-RAISING FLOUR
1 TEASPOON BICARBONATE OF SODA (BAKING SODA)
1 TEASPOON MIXED SPICE
2 TEASPOONS ICING (CONFECTIONERS') SUGAR

LEMON CREAM CHEESE FILLING

100G (3 OUNCES) CREAM CHEESE, SOFTENED
1 TEASPOON FINELY GRATED LEMON RIND
1 CUP (160G) ICING (CONFECTIONERS') SUGAR

1 Preheat oven to 200°C/400°F. Grease oven trays; line with baking paper.

2 Beat butter, brown sugar and egg in a medium bowl with an electric mixer until light and fluffy. Stir in banana, buttermilk and sifted flours, soda and spice.

3 Drop level tablespoons of mixture about 5cm (2 inches) apart onto trays; tap trays lightly on the bench to spread slightly.

4 Bake cakes about 10 minutes. Cool on trays.

5 Meanwhile, make lemon cream cheese filling.

6 Sandwich cakes with filling; dust with icing sugar.

lemon cream cheese filling Beat ingredients in a small bowl with an electric mixer until smooth.

tips You need 1 small overripe banana (130g) for the amount of mashed banana used in this recipe. Unfilled cakes can be frozen for up to 2 months. Kisses, once filled, should be served within several hours.

GINGER

& LIME KISSES

PREP + COOK TIME 45 MINUTES **MAKES** 20

125G (4 OUNCES) BUTTER, SOFTENED
⅔ CUP (150G) FIRMLY PACKED BROWN SUGAR
1 EGG
⅔ CUP (160ML) BUTTERMILK
½ CUP (40G) DESICCATED COCONUT
1¼ CUPS (185G) PLAIN (ALL-PURPOSE) FLOUR
¼ CUP (35G) SELF-RAISING FLOUR
1 TEASPOON BICARBONATE OF SODA (BAKING SODA)
1 TABLESPOON GROUND GINGER
¼ TEASPOON GROUND CLOVES

LIME BUTTER CREAM

100G (3 OUNCES) BUTTER, SOFTENED
1 TEASPOON FINELY GRATED LIME RIND
1 CUP (160G) ICING (CONFECTIONERS') SUGAR

1 Preheat oven to 200°C/400°F. Grease oven trays; line with baking paper.

2 Beat butter, sugar and egg in a medium bowl with an electric mixer until light and fluffy. Stir in buttermilk, coconut and sifted flours, soda and spices.

3 Drop level tablespoons of mixture about 5cm (2 inches) apart onto trays; tap trays lightly on the bench to spread slightly.

4 Bake cakes about 10 minutes. Cool on trays.

5 Meanwhile, make lime butter cream.

6 Sandwich cakes with butter cream.

lime butter cream Beat butter in a small bowl with an electric mixer until as white as possible. Beat in rind and sifted icing sugar until smooth.

tip Unfilled cakes can be frozen for 2 months. Kisses, once filled, should be served within several hours.

CARAMEL APPLE KISSES

PREP + COOK TIME 45 MINUTES **MAKES** 20

125G (4 OUNCES) BUTTER, SOFTENED
⅓ CUP (75G) FIRMLY PACKED LIGHT BROWN SUGAR
1 EGG
1 TABLESPOON TREACLE
⅔ CUP (160ML) BUTTERMILK
1 SMALL GREEN-SKINNED APPLE (130G)
1¼ CUPS (185G) PLAIN (ALL-PURPOSE) FLOUR
¼ CUP (35G) SELF-RAISING FLOUR
1 TEASPOON BICARBONATE OF SODA (BAKING SODA)
½ CUP (125ML) THICKENED (HEAVY) CREAM
⅓ CUP (110G) CARAMEL TOP 'N' FILL

1 Preheat oven to 200°C/400°F. Grease oven trays; line with baking paper.
2 Beat butter, sugar, egg and treacle in a medium bowl with an electric mixer until light and fluffy. Stir in buttermilk, coarsely grated apple and combined sifted flours and soda.
3 Drop level tablespoons of mixture about 5cm (2 inches) apart onto trays; tap trays lightly on the bench to spread slightly.
4 Bake cakes about 10 minutes. Cool on trays.
5 Meanwhile, beat cream in a small bowl with the electric mixer until firm peaks form.
6 Sandwich cakes with caramel and cream.
tip Unfilled cakes can be frozen for 2 months. Kisses, once filled, should be served within several hours.

WHITE CHOCOLATE & PASSIONFRUIT KISSES

PREP + COOK TIME 50 MINUTES **MAKES** 20

125G (4 OUNCES) UNSALTED BUTTER, SOFTENED
½ CUP (110G) CASTER (SUPERFINE) SUGAR
1 EGG
1¼ CUPS (185G) PLAIN (ALL-PURPOSE) FLOUR
¼ CUP (35G) SELF-RAISING FLOUR
1 TEASPOON BICARBONATE OF SODA (BAKING SODA)
½ CUP (125ML) BUTTERMILK
100G (3 OUNCES) WHITE CHOCOLATE, GRATED COARSELY
2 TABLESPOONS PASSIONFRUIT PULP
2 TABLESPOONS ICING (CONFECTIONERS') SUGAR

PASSIONFRUIT MARSHMALLOW FILLING

2 EGG WHITES
⅔ CUP (150G) CASTER (SUPERFINE) SUGAR
1 TABLESPOON GLUCOSE SYRUP
2 TABLESPOONS PASSIONFRUIT JUICE
YELLOW FOOD COLOURING

1 Preheat oven to 200°C/400°F. Grease oven trays; line with baking paper.

2 Beat butter, caster sugar and egg in a small bowl with an electric mixer until light and fluffy. Beat in sifted dry ingredients and buttermilk, on low speed, until smooth. Stir in white chocolate and passionfruit.

3 Drop level tablespoons of mixture about 5cm (2 inches) apart onto trays; tap trays lightly on the bench to spread slightly.

4 Bake cakes about 10 minutes. Cool on trays.

5 Meanwhile, make passionfruit marshmallow filling.

6 Spoon marshmallow filling into a piping bag fitted with a 2cm (¾-inch) fluted tube. Pipe filling on the flat side of half the cooled cakes; sandwich with remaining cakes. Serve kisses dusted with sifted icing sugar.

passionfruit marshmallow filling Place ingredients in a medium heatproof bowl over a medium saucepan of simmering water (do not allow water to touch base of bowl). Whisk vigorously for 10 minutes or until thick and creamy. Remove from heat; transfer mixture to a large heatproof bowl. Beat with electric mixer, on high speed, for 5 minutes or until mixture is thick and holds its shape.

tip Unfilled cakes can be frozen for 2 months. Kisses, once filled, should be served within several hours.

CHOCOLATE RASPBERRY KISSES

PREP + COOK TIME 1 HOUR MAKES 20

125G (4 OUNCES) UNSALTED BUTTER, SOFTENED
½ CUP (110G) FIRMLY PACKED BROWN SUGAR
1 EGG
¾ CUP (110G) PLAIN (ALL-PURPOSE) FLOUR
⅓ CUP (35G) COCOA POWDER
¼ CUP (35G) SELF-RAISING FLOUR
1 TEASPOON BICARBONATE OF SODA (BAKING SODA)
⅔ CUP (160ML) BUTTERMILK
125G (4 OUNCES) FRESH RASPBERRIES, TORN

RASPBERRY BUTTER CREAM

125G (4 OUNCES) UNSALTED BUTTER, SOFTENED
1½ CUPS (240G) ICING (CONFECTIONERS') SUGAR
1 TABLESPOON MILK
PINK FOOD COLOURING
2 TABLESPOONS RASPBERRY JAM

CHOCOLATE GANACHE

2 TABLESPOONS POURING CREAM
100G (3 OUNCES) DARK (SEMI-SWEET) CHOCOLATE, CHOPPED FINELY

1 Preheat oven to 200°C/400°F. Grease oven trays; line with baking paper.

2 Beat butter, sugar and egg in a small bowl with an electric mixer until light and fluffy. Beat in sifted dry ingredients and buttermilk, on low speed, until mixture is smooth.

3 Drop level tablespoons of mixture about 5cm (2 inches) apart onto trays. Bake cakes about 10 minutes. Cool on trays.

4 Meanwhile, make raspberry butter cream, then chocolate ganache.

5 Spoon butter cream into a piping bag fitted with a 2cm (¾-inch) fluted tube. Pipe butter cream on the flat side of half the cooled cakes.

6 Spread ganache over rounded side of remaining cooled cakes. Place on top of butter cream. Top kisses with raspberries.

raspberry butter cream Beat butter in a small bowl with an electric mixer until light and fluffy. Beat in sifted icing sugar and milk. Tint pink with colouring; stir in jam.

chocolate ganache Bring cream to the boil in a small saucepan. Remove from heat; stir in chocolate until smooth.

tip Unfilled cakes can be frozen for 2 months. Kisses, once filled, should be served within several hours.

ROSEWATER GLAZED MADELEINES

PREP + COOK TIME 35 MINUTES (+ COOLING) **MAKES** 24

125G (4 OUNCES) BUTTER, MELTED
1 TABLESPOON PLAIN (ALL-PURPOSE) FLOUR
2 EGGS
⅓ CUP (75G) CASTER (SUPERFINE) SUGAR
2 TEASPOONS ROSEWATER
1 TEASPOON VANILLA BEAN PASTE
⅔ CUP (100G) PLAIN (ALL-PURPOSE) FLOUR, EXTRA
¼ TEASPOON BAKING POWDER

GLACÉ ICING

1 CUP (160G) ICING (CONFECTIONERS') SUGAR
1 TEASPOON BUTTER
2 TABLESPOONS LEMON JUICE, APPROXIMATELY
PINK FOOD COLOURING

1 Preheat oven to 200°C/400°F. Brush two 12-hole (1½-tablespoon/30ml) madeleine pans with 1 tablespoon of the melted butter. Dust with the flour; shake out excess.

2 Beat eggs, sugar, rosewater and vanilla bean paste in a small bowl with an electric mixer for 5 minutes or until thick and creamy.

3 Sift extra flour and baking powder twice onto a piece of baking paper. Sift flour mixture a third time over egg mixture; fold into egg mixture with remaining melted butter. Drop tablespoons of mixture into pan holes.

4 Bake madeleines about 10 minutes. Leave madeleines in pans for 2 minutes before turning onto a wire rack to cool.

5 Meanwhile, make glacé icing.

6 Dip one end of each madeleine into icing; place on a baking-paper-covered wire rack for 5 minutes or until set.

glacé icing Sift icing sugar into a small heatproof bowl; stir in butter and enough juice to make a thick paste. Place the bowl over a small saucepan of simmering water; stir until icing is of a pouring consistency (do not overheat). Tint pink with colouring.

tip These madeleines are best eaten on the day they are made.

FROU FROU CUPCAKES

PREP + COOK TIME 1 HOUR **MAKES** 12

125G (4 OUNCES) BUTTER, SOFTENED
1 CUP (220G) CASTER (SUPERFINE) SUGAR
3 EGGS
½ CUP (75G) PLAIN (ALL-PURPOSE) FLOUR
¼ CUP (35G) SELF-RAISING FLOUR
½ CUP (40G) DESICCATED COCONUT
⅓ CUP (80G) SOUR CREAM
155G (5 OUNCES) FROZEN RASPBERRIES (SEE TIPS)
1 CUP (50G) FLAKED COCONUT, TOASTED
24 FRESH RASPBERRIES

CREAM CHEESE FROSTING

60G (2 OUNCES) BUTTER, SOFTENED
155G (5 OUNCES) CREAM CHEESE, SOFTENED
2 TEASPOONS COCONUT EXTRACT
3 CUPS (480G) ICING (CONFECTIONERS') SUGAR

1 Preheat oven to 180°C/350°F. Line a 12-hole (⅓-cup/80ml) muffin pan with paper cases.

2 Beat butter, sugar and eggs in a small bowl with an electric mixer until light and fluffy. Stir in sifted flours, desiccated coconut, sour cream and frozen raspberries. Spoon mixture into paper cases; smooth surface.

3 Bake cakes about 40 minutes. Leave cakes in pan for 5 minutes before turning, top-side up, onto a wire rack to cool. Remove paper cases from cold cakes.

4 Make cream cheese frosting.

5 Spread top and side of cakes with frosting; decorate with flaked coconut and fresh raspberries.

cream cheese frosting Beat butter, cream cheese and extract in a small bowl with an electric mixer until light and fluffy; gradually beat in sifted icing sugar.

tips Do not thaw the frozen raspberries as their colour will bleed into the cake. These cakes are best made on the day of serving. Unfrosted cakes can be frozen for up to 3 months.

CHOCOLATE HEART CUPCAKES

PREP + COOK TIME 1 HOUR (+ COOLING) **MAKES** 12

1 CUP (150G) SELF-RAISING FLOUR
½ CUP (75G) PLAIN (ALL-PURPOSE) FLOUR
⅓ CUP (35G) COCOA POWDER
¾ CUP (165G) CASTER (SUPERFINE) SUGAR
185G (6 OUNCES) BUTTER, SOFTENED
3 EGGS
½ CUP (125ML) MILK
1 TABLESPOON ICING (CONFECTIONERS') SUGAR

RASPBERRY FROSTING

40G (1½ OUNCES) BUTTER, SOFTENED
¼ CUP (40G) FROZEN RASPBERRIES, THAWED
1 CUP (160G) ICING (CONFECTIONERS') SUGAR

1 Preheat oven to 180°C/350°F. Line a 12-hole (⅓-cup/80ml) muffin pan with paper cases.

2 Sift flours and cocoa into a large bowl of an electric mixer, add caster sugar, butter, eggs and milk; beat on low speed until ingredients are combined. Increase speed to medium; beat until mixture is smooth and has changed to a paler colour. Drop ¼ cups of mixture into paper cases.

3 Bake cupcakes for about 20 minutes. Leave cakes in pan for 5 minutes before turning, top-side up, onto a wire rack to cool.

4 Make raspberry frosting.

5 Carefully cut the top off each cupcake. Using a 4cm (1½-inch) heart-shaped cutter, cut heart shapes from cake tops; reserve cake tops. Dust heart shapes with sifted icing sugar.

6 Spread 2 teaspoons of raspberry frosting over each cake. Replace cake tops, then top with hearts, using picture as a guide.

raspberry frosting Blend or process ingredients until smooth.

tips You need a 4cm (1½-inch) heart-shaped cutter. Uniced cakes can be made a day ahead or frozen for up to 3 months. Ice cakes on the day of serving.

ROSEWATER MERINGUE KISSES

PREP + COOK TIME 1¼ HOURS (+ COOLING & REFRIGERATION) MAKES 20

2 EGG WHITES
½ CUP (110G) CASTER (SUPERFINE) SUGAR
1 TEASPOON ROSEWATER
PINK FOOD COLOURING
2 TABLESPOONS POURING CREAM
90G (3 OUNCES) WHITE CHOCOLATE, CHOPPED FINELY
4 FRESH OR THAWED FROZEN RASPBERRIES

1 Preheat oven to 120°C/250°F. Grease oven trays; line with baking paper.
2 Beat egg whites, sugar, rosewater and a few drops of pink colouring in a small bowl with an electric mixer for 10 minutes or until sugar is dissolved.
3 Fit a large piping bag with a 2cm (¾-inch) plain tube. Paint three stripes of pink food colouring on the inside of the piping bag; spoon meringue mixture into bag. Pipe meringue into 4cm (1½-inch) rounds, about 2cm (¾ inch) apart, onto oven trays.
4 Bake meringues for 50 minutes or until dry to touch. Cool on trays.
5 Meanwhile, bring cream to the boil in a small saucepan. Remove from heat; stir in chocolate until smooth. Push raspberries through a fine sieve over a small bowl to make raspberry puree; you will need 2 teaspoons. Stir puree into chocolate mixture with a few drops of pink colouring. Refrigerate 20 minutes or until filling is spreadable.
6 Just before serving, sandwich meringues with filling.
tip You can paint any colour food colouring inside the piping bag. For multicoloured meringues paint a different colour for each stripe.

MULBERRY CREAM POWDER PUFFS

PREP + COOK TIME 1 HOUR (+ COOLING) **MAKES** 12

2 EGGS
⅓ CUP (75G) CASTER (SUPERFINE) SUGAR
2 TABLESPOONS CORNFLOUR (CORNSTARCH)
2 TABLESPOONS PLAIN (ALL-PURPOSE) FLOUR
2 TABLESPOONS SELF-RAISING FLOUR
1 TABLESPOON ICING (CONFECTIONERS') SUGAR
MULBERRY CREAM
½ CUP (125ML) THICKENED (HEAVY) CREAM
1 TABLESPOON ICING (CONFECTIONERS') SUGAR
½ CUP (70G) FINELY CHOPPED FRESH MULBERRIES

1 Preheat oven to 180°C/350°F. Butter and flour two 12-hole (1-tablespoon/20ml) shallow round-based patty pans.
2 Beat eggs and caster sugar in a small bowl with an electric mixer for 5 minutes or until thick and creamy. Sift flours twice onto baking paper, then sift a third time over egg mixture; fold flour into egg mixture. Drop level tablespoons of mixture into pan holes.
3 Bake cakes about 12 minutes; immediately turn onto wire racks to cool.
4 Make mulberry cream.
5 Just before serving, sandwich cakes with mulberry cream; dust with icing sugar.

mulberry cream Beat cream and sifted icing sugar in a small bowl with an electric mixer until soft peaks form; fold in berries.

tips Use any fresh berries you like in this recipe. If you only have one patty pan, bake the first batch, then wash, butter and flour the pan again before baking the next batch.

ROSEWATER RASPBERRY CUPCAKES

PREP + COOK TIME 1½ HOURS (+ COOLING) **MAKES** 12

YOU NEED 12 X 1¼-CUP (310ML) STRAIGHT-SIDED GLASS JARS.

3 CUPS (450G) SELF-RAISING FLOUR
250G (5½ OUNCES) BUTTER, SOFTENED
1 TEASPOON VANILLA EXTRACT
1½ CUPS (330G) CASTER (SUPERFINE) SUGAR
6 EGGS
½ CUP (125ML) MILK
ROSE PINK FOOD COLOURING
100G (3 OUNCES) PINK ROSE-FLAVOURED PERSIAN FAIRY FLOSS (PASHMAK)

ROSEWATER CREAM

600ML THICKENED (HEAVY) CREAM
½ TEASPOON ROSEWATER
ROSE PINK FOOD COLOURING

1 Preheat oven to 180°C/350°F.

2 Sift flour into a small bowl of an electric mixer, add butter, extract, sugar, eggs and milk; beat with an electric mixer on low speed until ingredients are combined. Increase speed to medium; beat until mixture is changed to a paler colour.

3 Divide mixture into three medium bowls. Tint one bowl pale pink with food colouring. Tint another bowl a medium shade of pink. Tint remaining bowl a darker pink. Spoon dark pink cake mixture into a plastic disposable piping bag; snip end to make a 1cm (½-inch) opening. Pipe mixture evenly into base of each jar, piping around the edge first, then in the middle (this will give you nice neat layers). Repeat with remaining mixtures and separate piping bags, finishing with the palest pink mixture.

4 Place jars in a large deep baking dish; pour enough boiling water into baking dish to come 3cm (1¼ inches) up the sides of jars. Cover dish with foil. Place dish in oven; bake about 50 minutes. Remove jars from dish; cool.

5 Just before serving, make rosewater cream. Dollop rosewater cream on top of cooled cakes in jars; top with fairy floss.

rosewater cream Combine cream and rosewater in a medium bowl of an electric mixer; tint pink with food colouring (tint slightly darker than you want, as the colour will become slightly less intense once you whip it). Beat mixture with an electric mixer until soft peaks form.

tip Swap the butter cake for 2 x 340g (11-ounce) packets butter cake mix if you like. Make the cakes according to packet directions.

CHAMPAGNE MINI CUPCAKES

PREP + COOK TIME 1½ HOURS (+ COOLING) **MAKES** 48

125G (4 OUNCES) BUTTER, SOFTENED
1 TEASPOON VANILLA EXTRACT
¾ CUP (165G) CASTER (SUPERFINE) SUGAR
3 EGGS
1½ CUPS (225G) SELF-RAISING FLOUR
¼ CUP (60ML) SPARKLING WINE
PINK SANDING SUGAR, TO DECORATE
PINK SOFT SUGAR PEARLS, TO DECORATE

CHAMPAGNE BUTTER CREAM
250G (8 OUNCES) BUTTER, SOFTENED
3 CUPS (480G) ICING (CONFECTIONERS') SUGAR
¼ CUP (60ML) SPARKLING WINE

1 Preheat oven to 180°C/350°F. Line four 12-hole (1-tablespoon/20ml) mini muffin pans with paper cases.
2 Beat butter, extract, sugar, eggs, sifted flour and wine in a small bowl with an electric mixer on low speed until ingredients are combined. Increase speed to medium; beat until mixture has changed to a paler colour. Drop 2 level teaspoons of mixture into each paper case.
3 Bake cupcakes about 12 minutes. Leave cakes in pan for 5 minutes before turning, top-side up, onto a wire rack to cool.
4 Make champagne butter cream.
5 Spoon butter cream into a large piping bag fitted with a large fluted tube. Pipe swirls of butter cream on top of each cake. Sprinkle with sanding sugar and sugar pearls.

champagne butter cream Beat butter in a small bowl with an electric mixer until as white as possible. Beat in sifted icing sugar and wine, in two batches.

tips Sanding sugar is a decorating sugar that adds colour and sparkle; it also holds its shape and colour after baking. It is available in a range of colours from specialist food and cake decorating stores. Uniced cakes can be made a day ahead or frozen for up to 3 months.

BLACKBERRY SWIRL LEMONADE CUPCAKES

PREP + COOK TIME 1 HOUR (+ COOLING) MAKES 12

125G (4 OUNCES) BUTTER, SOFTENED
½ CUP (110G) CASTER (SUPERFINE) SUGAR
1 TABLESPOON FINELY GRATED LEMON RIND
2 EGGS
1½ CUPS (225G) SELF-RAISING FLOUR
½ CUP (125ML) LEMONADE (SEE TIP)
12 FROZEN OR FRESH BLACKBERRIES

BLACKBERRY SWIRL FROSTING

¼ CUP (35G) FROZEN BLACKBERRIES, THAWED
500G (1 POUND) CREAM CHEESE, SOFTENED
2 CUPS (320G) ICING (CONFECTIONERS') SUGAR
1 TABLESPOON LEMONADE
2 TEASPOONS FINELY GRATED LEMON RIND

1 Preheat oven to 180°C/350°F. Line a 12-hole (⅓-cup/80ml) muffin pan with paper cases.

2 Meanwhile, make blackberry swirl frosting.

3 Beat butter, sugar and rind in a small bowl with an electric mixer until light and fluffy. Beat in eggs, one at a time. Transfer mixture to a large bowl; stir in sifted flour and lemonade, in two batches. Spoon mixture evenly into paper cases.

4 Bake cupcakes about 20 minutes. Leave cakes in pan for 5 minutes before turning, top-side up, onto wire racks to cool.

5 Just before serving, using a small ice-cream scoop, scoop frosting onto cupcakes.

blackberry swirl frosting Crush blackberries very well with a fork. Beat cream cheese, sifted icing sugar, lemonade and rind in a small bowl with an electric mixer until smooth. Lightly fold crushed berries through cream cheese mixture to create a swirled effect (don't over-mix or you will lose the swirl). Place frosting in the freezer for a few hours or until firm.

tip Use a clear, carbonated lemonade for this recipe.

MINI CHOCOLATE HAZELNUT CAKES

PREP + COOK TIME 55 MINUTES (+ STANDING & COOLING) **MAKES** 12

100G (3 OUNCES) DARK (SEMI-SWEET) CHOCOLATE, CHOPPED
¾ CUP (180ML) WATER
100G (3 OUNCES) BUTTER, SOFTENED
1 CUP (220G) FIRMLY PACKED BROWN SUGAR
3 EGGS
¼ CUP (25G) COCOA POWDER
¾ CUP (110G) SELF-RAISING FLOUR
⅓ CUP (35G) GROUND HAZELNUTS

WHIPPED HAZELNUT GANACHE

⅓ CUP (80ML) THICKENED (HEAVY) CREAM
180G (6 OUNCES) MILK CHOCOLATE, CHOPPED FINELY
2 TABLESPOONS HAZELNUT-FLAVOURED LIQUEUR

1 Preheat oven to 180°C/350°F. Grease two 6-hole (½-cup/125ml) oval friand pans.
2 Make whipped hazelnut ganache.
3 Stir chocolate and the water in a medium saucepan over low heat until smooth.
4 Beat butter and sugar in a small bowl with an electric mixer until light and fluffy. Beat in eggs, one at a time (the mixture might curdle at this stage, but will come together later). Transfer mixture to a medium bowl. Stir in warm chocolate mixture, sifted cocoa and flour, and nuts. Spoon mixture into pan holes.
5 Bake cakes about 20 minutes. Leave cakes in pan for 5 minutes before turning, top-side up, onto wire rack to cool.
6 Spread ganache on cakes.

whipped hazelnut ganache Stir cream and chocolate in a small saucepan over low heat until smooth; stir in liqueur. Transfer mixture to a small bowl. Cover; stand for 2 hours or until just firm. Beat ganache in a small bowl with the electric mixer until mixture changes to a pale brown colour.

CARAMEL CRUNCH
CHOCOLATE CUPCAKES

PREP + COOK TIME 1 HOUR (+ COOLING) **MAKES** 12

60G (2 OUNCES) DARK (SEMI-SWEET) CHOCOLATE, CHOPPED COARSELY
⅔ CUP (160ML) WATER
90G (3 OUNCES) BUTTER, SOFTENED
1 CUP (220G) FIRMLY PACKED BROWN SUGAR
2 EGGS
⅔ CUP (100G) SELF-RAISING FLOUR
2 TABLESPOONS COCOA POWDER
⅓ CUP (40G) GROUND ALMONDS
¾ CUP (180ML) GOOD-QUALITY STORE-BOUGHT CARAMEL SAUCE
¼ CUP (35G) FINELY CHOPPED SALTED PEANUTS

PEANUT BUTTER CREAM
¾ CUP (210G) SMOOTH OR CRUNCHY PEANUT BUTTER
185G (6 OUNCES) BUTTER, SOFTENED
1½ TABLESPOONS MILK
1¼ CUPS (200G) ICING (CONFECTIONERS') SUGAR

1 Preheat oven to 170°C/340°F. Line a 12-hole (⅓-cup/80ml) muffin pan with paper cases.
2 Stir chocolate and the water in a small saucepan over low heat until smooth.
3 Beat butter, sugar and eggs in a small bowl with an electric mixer until light and fluffy. Stir in sifted flour and cocoa, then ground almonds and warm chocolate mixture. Spoon mixture evenly into paper cases.
4 Bake cupcakes about 25 minutes. Leave cakes in pan for 5 minutes before turning, top-side up, onto a wire rack to cool.
5 Make peanut butter cream.
6 Cut a deep circle into the top of cold cakes; fill each hole with about 2 teaspoons of caramel sauce.
7 Spoon peanut butter cream into a large piping bag fitted with a large fluted tube; pipe swirls over caramel filling. Drizzle with remaining caramel sauce; sprinkle with nuts.

peanut butter cream Beat peanut butter, butter and milk in a small bowl with an electric mixer until light and fluffy. Gradually beat in sifted icing sugar.

tip Unfilled, uniced cakes can be made a day ahead or frozen for up to 3 months.

MINI BANANA BLUEBERRY CAKES

PREP + COOK TIME 50 MINUTES (+ COOLING) **MAKES** 24

125G (4 OUNCES) BUTTER, CHOPPED
½ CUP (125ML) MILK
2 EGGS
1 CUP (220G) CASTER (SUPERFINE) SUGAR
½ CUP MASHED BANANA
1½ CUPS (225G) SELF-RAISING FLOUR
1 CUP (150G) FROZEN BLUEBERRIES
1 TABLESPOON ICING (CONFECTIONERS') SUGAR

1 Preheat oven to 180°C/350°F. Grease two 12-hole (⅓-cup/80ml) muffin pans.
2 Place butter and milk in small saucepan; stir over low heat until butter melts. Cool to room temperature.
3 Beat eggs in a small bowl with an electric mixer until thick and creamy. Gradually add sugar, beating until dissolved after each addition; stir in banana. Fold in flour and cooled butter mixture, in two batches. Spoon mixture into pan holes.
4 Bake cakes 10 minutes. Remove pan from oven; press frozen blueberries into tops of cakes. Bake a further 10 minutes. Turn cakes, top-side up, onto a wire rack to cool. Just before serving, dust with icing sugar.
tips You will need 1 large overripe banana (230g) for the amount of mashed banana required in this recipe. Cakes can be stored in an airtight container for up to 3 days. Cakes are suitable to freeze for up to 1 month.

Cake

PATTY CAKES
WITH GLACÉ ICING

PREP + COOK TIME 45 MINUTES **MAKES** 12

125G (4 OUNCES) BUTTER, SOFTENED
¾ CUP (165G) CASTER (SUPERFINE) SUGAR
3 EGGS
½ TEASPOON VANILLA EXTRACT
2 CUPS (300G) SELF-RAISING FLOUR
¼ CUP (60ML) MILK
12 MARASCHINO CHERRIES

GLACÉ ICING

2 CUPS (320G) ICING (CONFECTIONERS') SUGAR
20G (¾ OUNCE) BUTTER, MELTED
2 TABLESPOONS HOT WATER, APPROXIMATELY
PINK AND GREEN FOOD COLOURING

1 Preheat oven to 180°C/350°F. Line a 12-hole (⅓-cup/80ml) muffin pan with paper cases.

2 Beat butter, sugar, eggs, extract, flour and milk in a medium bowl with an electric mixer on low speed until ingredients are combined. Increase speed to medium; beat for 3 minutes or until mixture is smooth and paler in colour.

3 Spoon mixture into paper cases. Bake cakes about 25 minutes. Leave cakes in pan for 5 minutes before turning, top-side up, onto a wire rack to cool.

4 Meanwhile, make glacé icing.

5 Spread cool cakes with icing; top each with a cherry.

glacé icing Sift icing sugar into a small bowl; stir in butter and enough of the water to make a firm paste. Place bowl over a small saucepan of simmering water; stir until icing is spreadable. Divide icing into two small bowls; tint one pink and the other green.

cake variations

berry & orange Stir in 1 teaspoon finely grated orange rind and ½ cup dried mixed berries at the end of step 2.

citrus Stir in ½ teaspoon each of finely grated lime, orange and lemon rind at the end of step 2.

passionfruit & white chocolate Stir in ¼ cup passionfruit pulp and ½ cup white Choc Bits at the end of step 2.

glacé icing variations

coconut & lime Stir in ½ teaspoon coconut essence and 1 teaspoon finely grated lime rind. Omit food colouring.

orange Stir in 1 teaspoon finely grated orange rind. Replace half the hot water with orange juice. Omit food colouring.

passionfruit Stir in 1 tablespoon passionfruit pulp. Omit food colouring.

NEAPOLITAN

SPLIT UNICED PATTY CAKES FROM PAGE 159, SANDWICH WITH A ROUND OF NEAPOLITAN ICE-CREAM. PIPE WHIPPED CREAM ON CAKE; DRIZZLE WITH CHOCOLATE SAUCE. DECORATE WITH PINK, WHITE AND CHOCOLATE SPRINKLES AND A MARASCHINO CHERRY.

HOKEY POKEY

SPLIT UNICED PATTY CAKES FROM PAGE 159, SANDWICH WITH A ROUND OF HOKEY POKEY ICE-CREAM. PIPE WHIPPED CREAM ON CAKES; DRIZZLE WITH CARAMEL SAUCE. DECORATE WITH CHOPPED HONEYCOMB AND A MARASCHINO CHERRY.

Ice-cream SANDWICHES

MINTY CHOC-CHIP

SPLIT UNICED PATTY CAKES FROM PAGE 159, SANDWICH WITH A ROUND OF CHOC-MINT ICE-CREAM. PIPE WHIPPED CREAM ON CAKES; DRIZZLE WITH CHOCOLATE SAUCE. DECORATE WITH CHOPPED PEPPERMINT CRISP BARS AND A MARASCHINO CHERRY.

CARAMEL CHOC SWIRL

SPLIT UNICED PATTY CAKES FROM PAGE 159, SANDWICH WITH A ROUND OF CARAMEL CHOCOLATE SWIRL ICE-CREAM. PIPE WHIPPED CREAM ON CAKE; DRIZZLE WITH CARAMEL SAUCE. DECORATE WITH CHOPPED JERSEY CARAMELS AND A MARASCHINO CHERRY.

PINK JELLY CAKES

PREP + COOK TIME 1¼ HOURS (+ COOLING & REFRIGERATION) MAKES 18

125G (4 OUNCES) BUTTER, SOFTENED
1 TEASPOON VANILLA EXTRACT
½ CUP (110G) CASTER (SUPERFINE) SUGAR
2 EGGS
1½ CUPS (225G) SELF-RAISING FLOUR
½ CUP (125ML) MILK
85G (3 OUNCE) PACKET RASPBERRY JELLY CRYSTALS
1 CUP (250ML) BOILING WATER
1 CUP (250ML) COLD WATER
½ CUP (125ML) THICKENED (HEAVY) CREAM
1 TABLESPOON ICING (CONFECTIONERS') SUGAR
2 CUPS (160G) DESICCATED COCONUT, APPROXIMATELY

1 Preheat oven to 200°C/400°F. Grease 18 holes of two 12-hole gem irons.

2 Beat butter, extract and sugar in a small bowl with an electric mixer until light and fluffy. Beat in eggs, one at a time, until combined. Stir in sifted flour and milk. Drop tablespoons of mixture into gem irons.

3 Bake cakes about 15 minutes. Turn cakes, top-side up, onto a wire rack to cool.

4 Meanwhile, dissolve jelly crystals in the boiling water; stir in the cold water until combined. Refrigerate for 45 minutes or until jelly is partly set.

5 Beat cream and icing sugar in a small bowl with the electric mixer until firm peaks form.

6 Cut rounded tops from cakes; join cakes with cream. Dip cakes in jelly, then roll in coconut. Place on a tray; refrigerate 30 minutes.

tip Old-fashioned gem irons, made from cast iron, are available from specialty cookware shops, or even second-hand shops.

COOKIES
& MORE

COLUMBIA

VANILLA BEAN THINS

PREP + COOK TIME 25 MINUTES **MAKES** 24

1 VANILLA BEAN
30G (1 OUNCE) BUTTER, SOFTENED
¼ CUP (55G) CASTER (SUPERFINE) SUGAR
1 EGG WHITE, BEATEN LIGHTLY
¼ CUP (35G) PLAIN (ALL-PURPOSE) FLOUR

1 Preheat oven to 200°C/400°F. Grease oven trays; line with baking paper.
2 Split vanilla bean lengthways; scrape seeds into a medium bowl, discard bean. Add butter and sugar to bowl; stir until combined. Stir in egg white and sifted flour.
3 Spoon mixture into a piping bag fitted with a 5mm (¼-inch) plain tube. Pipe 6cm (2½-inch) long strips (making them slightly wider at both ends) onto trays, about 5cm (2 inches) apart.
4 Bake biscuits for 5 minutes or until edges are browned lightly. Cool on trays.

CHOCOLATE CHIP COOKIES

PREP + COOK TIME 30 MINUTES **MAKES** 44

250G (8 OUNCES) BUTTER, SOFTENED
1 TEASPOON VANILLA EXTRACT
¾ CUP (165G) CASTER (SUPERFINE) SUGAR
¾ CUP (165G) FIRMLY PACKED BROWN SUGAR
1 EGG
2¼ CUPS (335G) PLAIN (ALL-PURPOSE) FLOUR
1 TEASPOON BICARBONATE OF SODA (BAKING SODA)
375G (12 OUNCES) DARK CHOCOLATE MELTS, CHOPPED COARSELY

1 Preheat oven to 180°C/350°F. Grease oven trays; line with baking paper.

2 Beat butter, extract, sugars and egg in a small bowl with an electric mixer until light and fluffy. Transfer mixture to a large bowl; stir in sifted flour and soda, in two batches. Stir in chocolate.

3 Roll tablespoons of mixture into balls; place on trays about 5cm (2 inches) apart.

4 Bake cookies for 15 minutes or until golden. Cool on trays.

tips For a more indulgent and intense chocolate taste, use a chocolate with 70% cocoa solids. For a chewier cookie, bake for 12 minutes. These cookies will keep in an airtight container for up to 1 week.

variations

milk choc Replace dark chocolate melts with milk or white chocolate melts.

choc nut Replace a third of the chocolate with roasted coarsely chopped nuts such as hazelnuts, walnuts, pecans or macadamias.

MINI JAM DROPS

PREP + COOK TIME 40 MINUTES MAKES 24

125G (4 OUNCES) BUTTER, SOFTENED
½ TEASPOON VANILLA EXTRACT
½ CUP (110G) CASTER (SUPERFINE) SUGAR
1 CUP (120G) GROUND ALMONDS
1 EGG
1 CUP (150G) PLAIN (ALL-PURPOSE) FLOUR
1 TEASPOON FINELY GRATED LEMON RIND
⅓ CUP (110G) RASPBERRY JAM
⅓ CUP (110G) APRICOT JAM

1 Preheat oven to 180°C/350°F. Line oven trays with baking paper.

2 Beat butter, extract, sugar and ground almonds in a small bowl with an electric mixer until light and fluffy. Beat in egg; stir in sifted flour.

3 Roll tablespoons of mixture into balls; place on trays about 5cm (2 inches) apart. Press a floured spoon or your thumb into the centre of each ball to make a hole.

4 Place raspberry and apricot jams in two small bowls. Divide rind between jams; mix well. Spoon jams into biscuit holes.

5 Bake biscuits about 15 minutes. Cool on trays.

tips You can use any fruit jams you like; strawberry would also work well in this recipe. Jam drops will keep in an airtight container for up to 2 days.

MELTING MOMENTS

PREP + COOK TIME 40 MINUTES MAKES 25

250G (8 OUNCES) BUTTER, SOFTENED
1 TEASPOON VANILLA EXTRACT
½ CUP (80G) ICING (CONFECTIONERS') SUGAR
1½ CUPS (225G) PLAIN (ALL-PURPOSE) FLOUR
½ CUP (75G) CORNFLOUR (CORNSTARCH)

BUTTER CREAM

90G (3 OUNCES) BUTTER, SOFTENED
¾ CUP (120G) ICING (CONFECTIONERS') SUGAR
1 TEASPOON FINELY GRATED LEMON RIND
1 TEASPOON LEMON JUICE

1 Preheat oven to 160°C/325°F. Line oven trays with baking paper.

2 Beat butter, extract and icing sugar in a small bowl with an electric mixer until light and fluffy. Transfer mixture to a large bowl; stir in combined sifted flours, in two batches.

3 With floured hands, roll rounded teaspoons of mixture into balls; place on trays about 2.5cm (1 inch) apart. Flatten slightly with a floured fork.

4 Bake biscuits about 15 minutes. Leave biscuits on tray for 5 minutes before lifting onto wire racks to cool.

5 Meanwhile, make butter cream.

6 Sandwich biscuits with butter cream. Just before serving, dust with a little more sifted icing sugar.

butter cream Beat butter, icing sugar and rind in a small bowl with the electric mixer until pale and fluffy; beat in juice.

tip Unfilled biscuits will keep in an airtight container for up to a week. Filled biscuits will keep for a few days in an airtight container in the fridge.

COCONUT MACAROONS

PREP + COOK TIME 50 MINUTES **MAKES** 24

2 EGG WHITES
½ CUP (110G) CASTER (SUPERFINE) SUGAR
1 TEASPOON VANILLA EXTRACT
¼ CUP (35G) PLAIN (ALL-PURPOSE) FLOUR
1½ CUPS (120G) DESICCATED COCONUT

1 Preheat oven to 150°C/300°F. Grease oven trays; line with baking paper.
2 Beat egg whites in a small bowl with an electric mixer until soft peaks form. Gradually add sugar, beating until dissolved after each addition. Stir in extract, sifted flour and coconut, in two batches.
3 Drop level tablespoons of the mixture onto trays about 5cm (2 inches) apart.
4 Bake macaroons for 25 minutes. Cool on trays.
tip These macaroons will keep in an airtight container for about a week.

ANZAC BISCUITS

PREP + COOK TIME 40 MINUTES MAKES 30

1 CUP (180G) ROLLED OATS
1 CUP (150G) PLAIN (ALL-PURPOSE) FLOUR
1 CUP (220G) CASTER (SUPERFINE) SUGAR
¾ CUP (60G) DESICCATED COCONUT
125G (4 OUNCES) BUTTER, CHOPPED
2 TABLESPOONS GOLDEN SYRUP OR TREACLE
1 TEASPOON BICARBONATE OF SODA (BAKING SODA)
2 TABLESPOONS BOILING WATER

1 Preheat oven to 150°C/300°F. Grease oven trays.
2 Combine oats, sifted flour, sugar and coconut in a large bowl.
3 Stir butter and golden syrup in a small saucepan over low heat until butter is melted.
4 Combine soda and water, add to butter mixture; stir into dry ingredients while mixture is warm.
5 Place 3-level-teaspoon portions of mixture onto trays about 4cm (1½ inches) apart; press down lightly.
6 Bake biscuits for 20 minutes or until golden brown. Loosen biscuits while warm; cool on trays.

tips It is best to use the traditional oats, not the quick cooking oats in this recipe. These biscuits can be stored in an airtight container for up to 1 week.

HONEY JUMBLES

PREP + COOK TIME 25 MINUTES (+ REFRIGERATION) **MAKES** 40

60G (2 OUNCES) BUTTER
½ CUP (110G) FIRMLY PACKED BROWN SUGAR
¾ CUP (270G) GOLDEN SYRUP
1 EGG, BEATEN LIGHTLY
2½ CUPS (375G) PLAIN (ALL-PURPOSE) FLOUR
½ CUP (75G) SELF-RAISING FLOUR
½ TEASPOON BICARBONATE OF SODA (BAKING SODA)
1 TEASPOON GROUND CINNAMON
½ TEASPOON GROUND CLOVE
2 TEASPOONS GROUND GINGER
1 TEASPOON MIXED SPICE

ICING

1 EGG WHITE
1½ CUPS (240G) ICING (CONFECTIONERS') SUGAR
2 TEASPOONS PLAIN (ALL-PURPOSE) FLOUR
1 TABLESPOON LEMON JUICE, APPROXIMATELY
PINK FOOD COLOURING

1 Preheat oven to 160°C/325°F. Grease oven trays.

2 Stir butter, sugar and syrup in a medium saucepan over low heat until sugar dissolves. Cool for 10 minutes.

3 Transfer cooled mixture to a large bowl; stir in egg and sifted dry ingredients, in two batches. Knead dough on a floured surface until it loses its stickiness. Wrap in plastic wrap; refrigerate 30 minutes.

4 Divide dough into eight portions. Roll each portion into a 2cm (¾-inch) thick sausage; cut each sausage into five 6cm (2½-inch) lengths. Place on trays about 3cm (1¼ inches) apart; round ends with lightly floured fingers, flatten slightly.

5 Bake biscuits about 15 minutes. Cool on trays.

6 Meanwhile, make icing.

7 Spread cooled biscuits with pink and white icing.

icing Beat egg white lightly in a small bowl; gradually stir in sifted icing sugar and flour, then enough juice to make icing spreadable. Place half the mixture in another small bowl; tint with pink colouring. Keep icings covered with a damp tea towel while in use.

Freshly
BAKED
SINCE 1819

Freshly
BAKED
SINCE 1819

TRADITIONAL SHORTBREAD

PREP + COOK TIME 1 HOUR MAKES 24

250G (8 OUNCES) BUTTER, SOFTENED
⅓ CUP (75G) CASTER (SUPERFINE) SUGAR
1 TABLESPOON WATER
2 CUPS (300G) PLAIN (ALL-PURPOSE) FLOUR
½ CUP (100G) RICE FLOUR
2 TABLESPOONS WHITE (GRANULATED) SUGAR

1 Preheat oven to 160°C/325°F. Grease two oven trays.
2 Beat butter and caster sugar in a medium bowl with an electric mixer until light and fluffy. Stir in the water and sifted flours, in two batches. Knead on a floured surface until smooth.
3 Divide dough in half; shape each, on separate trays, into a 20cm (8-inch) round. Mark each round into 12 wedges; prick with a fork. Pinch edges of rounds with your fingers; sprinkle with white sugar.
4 Bake shortbread about 40 minutes. Leave shortbread on trays for 5 minutes. Using a sharp knife, cut rounds into wedges along marked lines. Cool on trays.

tips We found that using half regular (salted) and half unsalted butter in shortbread recipes achieved the taste we liked best. Shortbread should be quite pale in colour after it's cooked. The rice flour is the ingredient that makes shortbread 'short' – a particular hard-to-describe mouth-feel.

MONTE CARLO BISCUITS

PREP + COOK TIME 40 MINUTES **MAKES** 30

180G (5½ OUNCES) BUTTER, SOFTENED
1 TEASPOON VANILLA EXTRACT
½ CUP (110G) FIRMLY PACKED BROWN SUGAR
1 EGG
1¼ CUPS (185G) SELF-RAISING FLOUR
¾ CUP (105G) PLAIN (ALL-PURPOSE) FLOUR
¼ TEASPOON BICARBONATE OF SODA (BAKING SODA)
⅔ CUP (50G) DESICCATED COCONUT
⅓ CUP (110G) RASPBERRY JAM
VIENNA CREAM
60G (2 OUNCES) BUTTER, SOFTENED
½ TEASPOON VANILLA EXTRACT
¾ CUP (120G) ICING (CONFECTIONERS') SUGAR
2 TEASPOONS MILK

1 Preheat oven to 200°C/400°F. Grease oven trays; line with baking paper.
2 Beat butter, extract and sugar in a small bowl with an electric mixer until just combined. Beat in egg. Stir in sifted flours, soda and coconut, in two batches.
3 Roll 2 level teaspoons of mixture into ovals; place on trays about 5cm (2 inches) apart. Flatten slightly; use back of fork to roughen surface.
4 Bake biscuits about 7 minutes. Lift biscuits onto a wire rack to cool.
5 Meanwhile, make vienna cream.
6 Sandwich biscuits with vienna cream and jam.
vienna cream Beat butter, extract and sifted icing sugar in a small bowl with the electric mixer until fluffy; beat in milk.

CHOCOLATE WHEATIES

PREP + COOK TIME 35 MINUTES **MAKES** 35

90G (3 OUNCES) BUTTER, SOFTENED
½ CUP (100G) FIRMLY PACKED BROWN SUGAR
1 EGG, BEATEN LIGHTLY
¼ CUP (20G) DESICCATED COCONUT
¼ CUP (25G) WHEATGERM
¾ CUP (120G) WHOLEMEAL PLAIN (ALL-PURPOSE) FLOUR
½ CUP (75G) WHITE SELF-RAISING FLOUR
150G (4½ OUNCES) DARK (SEMI-SWEET) CHOCOLATE, MELTED

1 Preheat oven to 180°C/350°F. Grease oven trays.
2 Beat butter and sugar in a small bowl with an electric mixer until smooth. Beat in egg. Stir in coconut, wheatgerm and sifted flours.
3 Roll rounded teaspoons of mixture into balls; place on trays about 3cm (1¼ inches) apart. Flatten with a floured fork.
4 Bake biscuits for 12 minutes or until lightly browned. Cool on trays.
5 Dip half of each biscuit in melted chocolate; place on wire racks, leave until set.
tip These biscuits can be stored in an airtight container for up to 1 week.

WHITE CHOCOLATE MACADAMIA COOKIES

PREP + COOK TIME 30 MINUTES **MAKES** 24

1½ CUPS (225G) PLAIN (ALL-PURPOSE) FLOUR
½ TEASPOON BICARBONATE OF SODA (BAKING SODA)
¼ CUP (55G) CASTER (SUPERFINE) SUGAR
⅓ CUP (75G) FIRMLY PACKED BROWN SUGAR
125G (4 OUNCES) BUTTER, MELTED
½ TEASPOON VANILLA EXTRACT
1 EGG
180G (6 OUNCES) WHITE CHOC BITS
¾ CUP (105G) ROASTED MACADAMIAS, CHOPPED COARSELY

1 Preheat oven to 200°C/400°F. Line two oven trays with baking paper.
2 Sift flour, soda and sugars into a large bowl. Stir in butter, extract and egg, then chocolate and nuts.
3 Drop rounded tablespoons of mixture on trays, about 5cm (2 inches) apart.
4 Bake cookies about 10 minutes. Cool on trays.

tips To roast macadamias, spead evenly on an oven tray and place in a 180°C/350°F oven for about 5 minutes. You can also stir them in a heavy-based frying pan over low heat. The natural oils will help turn them golden brown. These cookies can be stored in an airtight container for up to 1 week.

GINGERBREAD PEOPLE

PREP + COOK TIME 1 HOUR (+ REFRIGERATION) MAKES 16

125G (4 OUNCES) BUTTER
½ CUP (100G) FIRMLY PACKED BROWN SUGAR
1 EGG YOLK
2½ CUPS (375G) PLAIN (ALL-PURPOSE) FLOUR
1 TEASPOON BICARBONATE OF SODA (BAKING SODA)
3 TEASPOONS GROUND GINGER
½ CUP (125ML) GOLDEN SYRUP

ROYAL ICING

1 EGG WHITE
1½ CUPS (240G) PURE ICING (CONFECTIONERS') SUGAR, APPROXIMATELY
FOOD COLOURINGS

1 Preheat oven to 180°C/350°F. Grease oven trays.

2 Beat butter, sugar and egg yolk in a small bowl with an electric mixer until smooth. Stir in sifted dry ingredients and golden syrup to a soft dough. Knead dough on a floured surface until smooth. Roll dough between sheets of baking paper until 3mm (⅛-inch) thick. Refrigerate 1 hour.

3 Using a 13cm (5¼-inch) gingerbread-man cutter, cut out shapes from dough; place on trays about 3cm (1¼ inches) apart.

4 Bake gingerbread for 10 minutes or until lightly browned. Cool on trays.

5 Meanwhile, make royal icing.

6 Spoon icing into a piping bag fitted with a small plain tube; decorate shapes as desired.

royal icing Beat egg white in a small bowl with electric mixer until frothy; gradually beat in enough sifted icing sugar to give a mixture of piping consistency. Tint with colourings as desired. Keep royal icing covered with a damp tea towel to prevent icing drying out.

tip Gingerbread men cutters are available from kitchenware shops.

HONEY LEMON BISCUITS

PREP + COOK TIME 45 MINUTES (+ COOLING & STANDING) **MAKES** ABOUT 24

60G (2 OUNCES) BUTTER
¼ CUP (90G) HONEY
1 CUP (160G) WHOLEMEAL SELF-RAISING FLOUR
¼ CUP (35G) WHITE PLAIN (ALL-PURPOSE) FLOUR
½ TEASPOON GROUND CINNAMON
½ TEASPOON GROUND GINGER
¼ CUP (15G) UNPROCESSED WHEAT BRAN
1 TEASPOON WATER, APPROXIMATELY

ICING

⅔ CUP (110G) ICING (CONFECTIONERS') SUGAR
1 TEASPOON HONEY
2 TEASPOONS LEMON JUICE, APPROXIMATELY

1 Preheat oven to 180°C/350°F. Grease oven trays.

2 Beat butter and honey in a small bowl with an electric mixer until smooth. Stir in sifted dry ingredients, bran and enough water to mix to a soft dough.

3 Knead dough on a floured surface until smooth. Roll dough between sheets of baking paper until 3mm (⅛-inch) thick. Using a 5cm (2-inch) round fluted cutter, cut rounds from dough; place on trays about 3cm (1¼ inches) apart.

4 Bake biscuits for 10 minutes or until browned lightly. Leave biscuits on trays for 5 minutes before transferring to wire racks to cool.

5 Meanwhile, make icing.

6 Spread biscuits with icing; leave to set on wire racks.

icing Sift icing sugar into a small heatproof bowl; stir in honey and enough juice to make a stiff paste. Place bowl over a small saucepan of simmering water; stir until icing is spreadable.

SUGAR 'N' SPICE COOKIES

PREP + COOK TIME 30 MINUTES MAKES ABOUT 30

125G (4 OUNCES) BUTTER, SOFTENED
½ TEASPOON VANILLA EXTRACT
⅓ CUP (75G) RAW SUGAR
1 EGG
2 TABLESPOONS WHEATGERM
1 CUP (160G) WHOLEMEAL PLAIN (ALL-PURPOSE) FLOUR
2 TABLESPOONS WHOLEMEAL SELF-RAISING FLOUR
⅓ CUP (75G) RAW SUGAR, EXTRA
1 TEASPOON GROUND CINNAMON

1 Preheat oven to 180°C/350°F. Grease oven trays.

2 Beat butter, extract, sugar and egg in a small bowl with an electric mixer until smooth. Stir in wheatgerm and sifted flours.

3 Roll rounded teaspoons of mixture into balls; toss in combined extra sugar and cinnamon.

4 Place balls on trays about 3cm (1¼ inches) apart; flatten with a floured fork.

5 Bake cookies for 12 minutes or until lightly browned. Leave on trays for 5 minutes before transferring to wire racks to cool.

tip These cookies can be stored in an airtight container for up to 1 week.

WAFER ROLL BISCUITS

PREP + COOK TIME 50 MINUTES MAKES 28

COOK ONE TRAY OF WAFER ROLLS AT A TIME FOR EASY HANDLING.

2 EGG WHITES
⅓ CUP (75G) CASTER (SUPERFINE) SUGAR
¼ CUP (35G) PLAIN (ALL-PURPOSE) FLOUR
¼ TEASPOON MIXED SPICE
¼ TEASPOON GROUND GINGER
40G (1½ OUNCES) BUTTER, MELTED
1 TEASPOON CINNAMON SUGAR

1 Preheat oven to 180°C/350°F. Grease two oven trays. Mark four 8.5cm (3½-inch) circles on two sheets of baking paper; place on trays, marked-side down.
2 Beat egg whites in a small bowl with an electric mixer until soft peaks form. Gradually add sugar, beating until dissolved after each addition. Fold in sifted flour and spices, then butter.
3 Drop rounded teaspoons of mixture into marked circles, spread evenly to fill circles. Sprinkle each circle with a pinch of cinnamon sugar.
4 Bake one tray of biscuits at a time, for 4 minutes or until lightly browned. Working quickly with one circle at a time, slide a metal spatula under circle then roll around a plastic chopstick; leave to firm. Repeat process with remaining circles.

tips Cinnamon sugar is available in the spice section of most supermarkets. Wafer rolls are best made on day of serving. For other wafer roll ideas, see Sundae Toppings on pages 198 & 199.

GINGER & PECAN

HALF DIP WAFER ROLL BISCUITS FROM PAGE 197 IN MELTED DARK CHOCOLATE, THEN COAT IN FINELY CHOPPED GLACÉ GINGER; LEAVE TO SET. SERVE WAFERS WITH SCOOPS OF VANILLA ICE-CREAM, TOPPED WITH GINGER SYRUP AND CHOPPED ROASTED PECANS.

CLASSIC SUNDAE

HALF DIP WAFER ROLL BISCUITS FROM PAGE 197 IN MELTED MILK CHOCOLATE, THEN COAT IN HUNDREDS AND THOUSANDS; LEAVE TO SET. SERVE WAFERS WITH SCOOPS OF VANILLA ICE-CREAM, TOPPED WITH STRAWBERRY TOPPING, EXTRA HUNDREDS AND THOUSANDS AND MARASCHINO CHERRIES.

ROCKY ROAD

HALF DIP WAFER ROLL BISCUITS FROM PAGE 197 IN MELTED DARK CHOCOLATE, THEN COAT IN CHOPPED ROASTED PEANUTS; LEAVE TO SET. SERVE WAFERS WITH SCOOPS OF VANILLA ICE-CREAM, TOPPED WITH CHOCOLATE SAUCE, MINI MARSHMALLOWS AND EXTRA CHOPPED PEANUTS.

Sundae TOPPINGS

BANANA SPLIT

HALF DIP WAFER ROLL BISCUITS FROM PAGE 197 IN MELTED MILK CHOCOLATE, THEN COAT IN CHOPPED VIENNA ALMONDS; LEAVE TO SET. SERVE WAFERS WITH SCOOPS OF VANILLA ICE-CREAM WITH SLICED BANANA, CARAMEL SAUCE AND EXTRA CHOPPED ALMONDS.

BROWNIES & SLICES

CHOCOLATE CARAMEL SLICE

PREP + COOK TIME 55 MINUTES (+ REFRIGERATION) **MAKES** 48

1 CUP (150G) PLAIN (ALL-PURPOSE) FLOUR
½ CUP (110G) FIRMLY PACKED BROWN SUGAR
½ CUP (40G) DESICCATED COCONUT
125G (4 OUNCES) BUTTER, MELTED
60G (2 OUNCES) BUTTER, EXTRA
395G (12½ OUNCES) CANNED SWEETENED CONDENSED MILK
2 TABLESPOONS GOLDEN SYRUP OR TREACLE
185G (6 OUNCES) DARK (SEMI-SWEET) CHOCOLATE, CHOPPED COARSELY
2 TEASPOONS VEGETABLE OIL

1 Preheat oven to 180°C/350°F. Grease a 20cm x 30cm (8-inch x 12-inch) rectangular pan; line base and long sides with baking paper, extending the paper 5cm (2 inches) over sides.

2 Combine sifted flour, sugar and coconut in a medium bowl; stir in melted butter. Press mixture firmly over base of pan. Bake base about 15 minutes. Cool.

3 Place extra butter, condensed milk and syrup in a medium saucepan; stir over low heat until smooth. Pour mixture over base. Bake for 15 minutes or until golden brown. Cool.

4 Place chocolate and oil in a medium heatproof bowl over a medium saucepan of simmering water (make sure the water doesn't touch base of bowl); stir until smooth. Spread chocolate mixture over slice. Refrigerate for 30 minutes or until set before cutting with a hot knife.

tip This slice will keep in an airtight container for up to 1 week. If the weather is hot, store the container in the fridge.

CHOCOLATE LAMINGTONS

PREP + COOK TIME 1¼ HOURS **MAKES** 16

6 EGGS
⅔ CUP (150G) CASTER (SUPERFINE) SUGAR
⅓ CUP (50G) CORNFLOUR (CORNSTARCH)
½ CUP (75G) PLAIN (ALL-PURPOSE) FLOUR
⅓ CUP (50G) SELF-RAISING FLOUR
2 CUPS (160G) DESICCATED COCONUT, APPROXIMATELY

CHOCOLATE ICING

3 CUPS (500G) ICING (CONFECTIONERS') SUGAR
½ CUP (50G) COCOA POWDER
15G (½ OUNCE) BUTTER, MELTED
⅔ CUP (160ML) MILK

1 Preheat oven to 180°C/350°F. Grease a deep 23cm (9-inch) square cake pan.

2 Beat eggs in a medium bowl with an electric mixer for 10 minutes or until thick and creamy. Gradually add sugar, beating until sugar dissolves after each addition. Fold in triple-sifted flours. Spread mixture into pan.

3 Bake cake about 30 minutes. Turn cake, top-side up, onto a wire rack to cool.

4 Make chocolate icing.

5 Cut cooled cake into 16 squares. Dip squares in icing, drain off excess; toss squares in coconut. Place lamingtons on a wire rack to set.

chocolate icing Sift icing sugar and cocoa into a large heatproof bowl; stir in butter and milk. Place bowl over a large saucepan of simmering water; stir until icing becomes a coating consistency.

tips The cake is easier to handle if it has been made the day before. Sponge or butter cake can be used. You can fill the lamingtons with jam and cream. Lamingtons can be stored in an airtight container for up to 2 days.

DREAM BARS

PREP + COOK TIME 50 MINUTES **MAKES** 16

90G (3 OUNCES) BUTTER, SOFTENED
⅓ CUP (65G) FIRMLY PACKED BROWN SUGAR
1 CUP (150G) PLAIN (ALL-PURPOSE) FLOUR
2 TABLESPOONS ICING (CONFECTIONERS') SUGAR

TOPPING

2 EGGS, BEATEN LIGHTLY
1 TEASPOON VANILLA EXTRACT
½ CUP (100G) FIRMLY PACKED BROWN SUGAR
1 TABLESPOON PLAIN (ALL-PURPOSE) FLOUR
½ TEASPOON BAKING POWDER
1½ CUPS (135G) DESICCATED COCONUT
1 CUP (320G) BOTTLED FRUIT MINCE

1 Preheat oven to 180°C/350°F. Grease a 20cm x 30cm (8-inch x 12-inch) rectangular pan; line base and long sides with baking paper, extending the paper 5cm (2 inches) over sides.

2 Beat butter and sugar in a small bowl with an electric mixer until smooth. Stir in sifted flour.

3 Press mixture over base of pan. Bake base for 10 minutes.

4 Meanwhile, make topping.

5 Spread topping on hot base; bake a further 30 minutes or until firm. Cool slice in pan. Just before serving, dust with sifted icing sugar.

topping Beat eggs, extract and sugar in a small bowl with the electric mixer until thick and creamy. Fold in sifted flour and baking powder; then coconut and fruit mince.

RASPBERRY COCONUT SLICE

PREP + COOK TIME 50 MINUTES MAKES 18

90G (3 OUNCES) BUTTER, SOFTENED
½ CUP (110G) CASTER (SUPERFINE) SUGAR
1 EGG
⅓ CUP (50G) SELF-RAISING FLOUR
⅔ CUP (100G) PLAIN (ALL-PURPOSE) FLOUR
½ CUP (160G) RASPBERRY JAM

COCONUT TOPPING

2 EGGS
⅓ CUP (75G) CASTER (SUPERFINE) SUGAR
2 CUPS (160G) DESICCATED COCONUT

1 Preheat oven to 180°C/350°F. Grease a 20cm x 30cm (8-inch x 12-inch) rectangular pan; line base and long sides with baking paper, extending the paper 5cm (2 inches) over sides.

2 Beat butter, sugar and egg in a small bowl with an electric mixer until light and fluffy. Stir in sifted flours, in two batches. Spread mixture over base of pan; spread jam evenly over mixture.

3 Make coconut topping; spread evenly over jam.

4 Bake slice for about 35 minutes. Cool in pan. Cut cooled slice into pieces.

coconut topping Whisk eggs lightly with a fork in a medium bowl; stir in sugar and coconut.

variation Replace raspberry jam with apricot jam; in the topping, replace 1 cup of the desiccated coconut with ground almonds.

DELIGHTFUL PETITS FOURS

PREP + COOK TIME 1½ HOURS (+ REFRIGERATION & STANDING) MAKES 15-20

4 EGGS
¾ CUP (165G) CASTER (SUPERFINE) SUGAR
⅔ CUP (100G) PLAIN (ALL-PURPOSE) FLOUR
⅓ CUP (50G) CORNFLOUR (CORNSTARCH)
½ TEASPOON BAKING POWDER
¾ CUP (240G) APRICOT JAM
2 TABLESPOONS HAZELNUT-FLAVOURED LIQUEUR
100G (3 OUNCES) MARZIPAN
500G (1 POUND) READY-MADE WHITE ICING, CHOPPED COARSELY
1 EGG WHITE
PINK AND GREEN FOOD COLOURING
½ CUP (75G) WHITE CHOCOLATE MELTS

1 Preheat oven to 180°C/350°F. Grease a 23cm x 33cm (9-inch x 13-inch) swiss roll pan; line base and all sides with two layers of baking paper, extending the paper 5cm (2 inches) over sides.

2 Beat eggs in a small bowl with an electric mixer for 8 minutes or until pale and thick. Gradually add sugar, beat until sugar dissolves. Fold in sifted dry ingredients. Pour mixture into pan. Bake cake about 15 minutes. Stand cake in pan for 5 minutes before turning, top-side up, onto a baking-paper-covered wire rack to cool; remove lining paper. Trim all edges of cake.

3 Heat jam and liqueur in a small saucepan until melted; strain into a small bowl.

4 Cut cake in half crossways, then split each half horizontally. Place one of the top cake layers, top-side down, onto a tray; brush cut surface evenly with a quarter of the jam mixture. Continue layering with cake and brushing with jam mixture, until all cake pieces are used; brush top with jam mixture. (When layering, use one of the cake bases, bottom-side up, as the top of the cake for a smooth top.)

5 Roll marzipan between sheets of baking paper until large enough to cover top of cake. Place on top of cake; invert onto a baking-paper-covered tray. Wrap sides of cake in plastic wrap. Top cake with baking paper, place another tray on paper. Weight with a brick or other heavy object; refrigerate overnight.

6 Remove brick, tray and top piece of paper; invert cake onto a board, so the marzipan is on top. Cut cake in half crossways. Cut one half into 3cm (1¼-inch) squares. Use a deep 3cm (1¼-inch) round cutter to cut the other cake half into 3cm (1¼-inch) rounds.

7 Place ready-made icing in a medium heatproof bowl over a medium saucepan of simmering water; stir until smooth. Stir in egg white, and a little water if needed, until the icing is the consistency of pouring cream. Working quickly, pour a third of the icing into a small bowl; tint with pink colouring. Pour half the remaining icing into another small bowl; tint with green colouring. Leave remaining icing white. Cover icings with plastic so they won't dry out.

8 Separate cakes into three lots; place one lot of cakes on a wire rack over a tray. Quickly pour pink icing over these cakes; spread icing around sides as each cake is iced. Return excess icing from the tray to heatproof bowl, reheat over simmering water, then pour over cakes until completely covered.

9 Repeat with remaining cakes and icing. Stand the cakes at room temperature until set.

10 Gently melt chocolate; cool slightly (it must still be melted, but not hot, otherwise it will melt the icing). Spoon chocolate into a piping bag fitted with a small plain tube; decorate petit fours with chocolate. Stand until set.

CHOCOLATE ALMOND FINGERS

PREP + COOK TIME 45 MINUTES (+ COOLING & STANDING) **MAKES** 25

60G (2 OUNCES) BUTTER, SOFTENED
1 CUP (125G) GROUND ALMONDS
½ CUP (110G) CASTER (SUPERFINE) SUGAR
2 EGGS, BEATEN LIGHTLY
2 TABLESPOONS PLAIN (ALL-PURPOSE) FLOUR
100G (3 OUNCES) DARK (SEMI-SWEET) CHOCOLATE
1 TEASPOON VEGETABLE OIL

ALMOND TOPPING

60G (2 OUNCES) BUTTER, CHOPPED
⅓ CUP (75G) CASTER (SUPERFINE) SUGAR
⅓ CUP (80ML) GLUCOSE SYRUP
1½ CUPS (120G) FLAKED ALMONDS
2 TABLESPOONS WATER

1 Preheat oven to 200°C/400°F. Grease a 23cm x 33cm (9-inch x 13-inch) swiss roll pan; line base and long sides with baking paper, extending the paper 5cm (2 inches) over sides.

2 Beat butter, ground almonds and sugar in a small bowl with an electric mixer until smooth. Beat in eggs, one at a time. Stir in sifted flour until combined. Spread mixture over base of pan.

3 Bake base about 10 minutes; cool 5 minutes.

4 Meanwhile, make almond topping.

5 Spread topping on base; bake a further 10 minutes or until browned lightly. Cut while warm; lift onto wire racks to cool.

6 Place chocolate in a small heatproof bowl over a small saucepan of simmering water (make sure the water doesn't touch the base of the bowl); stir until melted. Combine melted chocolate and oil. Dip biscuits diagonally into chocolate mixture; place on wire racks, leave until set.

almond topping Stir ingredients in a medium saucepan over heat, without boiling, until sugar is dissolved. Bring to the boil; simmer, uncovered, without stirring, for 4 minutes or until thickened slightly.

CARAMEL WALNUT SLICE

PREP + COOK TIME 50 MINUTES MAKES 24

1 CUP (150G) SELF-RAISING FLOUR
1 CUP (80G) DESICCATED COCONUT
½ CUP (110G) CASTER (SUPERFINE) SUGAR
125G (4 OUNCES) BUTTER, MELTED

COCONUT WALNUT TOPPING

2 EGGS, BEATEN LIGHTLY
1 TEASPOON VANILLA EXTRACT
1 CUP (80G) DESICCATED COCONUT
¾ CUP (165G) FIRMLY PACKED BROWN SUGAR
½ CUP (60G) COARSELY CHOPPED WALNUTS

1 Preheat oven to 180°C/350°F. Grease a 20cm x 30cm (8-inch x 12-inch) rectangular pan; line base and long sides with baking paper, extending the paper 5cm (2 inches) over sides.

2 Combine sifted flour, coconut and sugar in a medium bowl; stir in butter. Press mixture into pan.

3 Bake base for 15 minutes.

4 Make coconut walnut topping; spread over base.

5 Bake slice a further 20 minutes. Cool slice in pan before cutting.

coconut walnut topping Combine eggs and extract in medium bowl; stir in coconut, sugar and walnuts.

tip This slice can be stored in an airtight container for up to 4 days.

FRUIT CHEW SQUARES

PREP + COOK TIME 55 MINUTES (+ COOLING) **MAKES** 24

90G (3 OUNCES) BUTTER, CHOPPED
⅓ CUP (75G) FIRMLY PACKED BROWN SUGAR
1¼ CUPS (185G) PLAIN (ALL-PURPOSE) FLOUR
1 EGG YOLK

FRUIT AND NUT TOPPING
2 EGGS
1 CUP (220G) FIRMLY PACKED LIGHT BROWN SUGAR
⅓ CUP (50G) SELF-RAISING FLOUR
½ CUP (85G) RAISINS
¾ CUP (120G) SULTANAS
1¼ CUPS (185G) ROASTED UNSALTED PEANUTS
1 CUP (80G) DESICCATED COCONUT

1 Preheat oven to 180°C/350°F. Grease a 20cm x 30cm (8-inch x 12-inch) rectangular pan; line base and long sides with baking paper, extending the paper 5cm (2 inches) over sides.
2 Stir butter and sugar in a medium saucepan over medium heat until butter is melted. Stir in sifted flour and egg yolk. Press mixture over base of pan.
3 Bake for 10 minutes or until browned lightly; cool.
4 Make fruit and nut topping.
5 Spread topping over cooled base; bake for a further 30 minutes or until browned lightly. Cool in pan before cutting into 24 pieces.

fruit and nut topping Beat eggs and sugar in a small bowl with an electric mixer until changed to a lighter colour and thickened slightly; fold in sifted flour. Transfer mixture to a large bowl; stir in remaining ingredients.

tips Brown sugar gives this nutty slice the colour and taste of caramel. This slice can be stored in an airtight container for up to 1 week.

Cakes

CHOCOLATE
HAZELNUT SLICE

PREP + COOK TIME 1¼ HOURS (+ COOLING & REFRIGERATION) **MAKES** 24

250G (8 OUNCES) PLAIN CHOCOLATE BISCUITS (SEE TIPS)
60G (2 OUNCES) BUTTER, MELTED
4 EGGS, SEPARATED (SEE TIPS)
¾ CUP (165G) CASTER (SUPERFINE) SUGAR
½ CUP (50G) GROUND HAZELNUTS
2 TABLESPOONS PLAIN (ALL-PURPOSE) FLOUR
1 TABLESPOON COCOA POWDER
CHOCOLATE TOPPING
125G (4 OUNCES) BUTTER, SOFTENED
½ CUP (110G) CASTER (SUPERFINE) SUGAR
1 TABLESPOON ORANGE JUICE
200G (6½ OUNCES) DARK (SEMI-SWEET) CHOCOLATE, MELTED

1 Preheat oven to 180°C/350°F. Grease a 20cm x 30cm (8-inch x 12-inch) rectangular pan; line base and long sides with baking paper, extending the paper 5cm (2 inches) over sides.
2 Process biscuits until fine. Combine 1 cup of the biscuit crumbs with butter in a medium bowl; press over base of pan. Refrigerate for 10 minutes.
3 Beat egg whites in a small bowl with an electric mixer until soft peaks form. Gradually add sugar, beating until dissolved after each addition; fold in hazelnuts, remaining biscuit crumbs and sifted flour. Spread mixture over biscuit base.
4 Bake base about 20 minutes. Cool 20 minutes.
5 Reduce oven to 160°C/325°F; make chocolate topping.
6 Spread topping over slice; bake slice a further 20 minutes. Cool in pan. Refrigerate until firm. Dust with sifted cocoa before cutting into 24 pieces.

chocolate topping Beat butter, sugar, egg yolks and juice in a small bowl with electric mixer until light and fluffy. Stir in melted chocolate.

tips Buy plain chocolate biscuits for this recipe, that is, without filling, icing or chocolate coating. The eggs are used in the biscuit base (whites) and the chocolate topping (yolks). This slice can be stored in an airtight container in the fridge for up to 1 week.

TANGY LEMON SQUARES

PREP + COOK TIME 55 MINUTES (+ COOLING) MAKES 16

125G (4 OUNCES) BUTTER, SOFTENED
¼ CUP (40G) ICING (CONFECTIONERS') SUGAR
1¼ CUPS (185G) PLAIN (ALL-PURPOSE) FLOUR
3 EGGS
1 CUP (220G) CASTER (SUPERFINE) SUGAR
2 TEASPOONS FINELY GRATED LEMON RIND
½ CUP (125ML) LEMON JUICE
2 TEASPOONS ICING (CONFECTIONERS') SUGAR, EXTRA

1 Preheat oven to 180°C/350°F. Grease a shallow 22cm (9-inch) square cake pan; line base and sides with baking paper, extending the paper 2.5cm (1 inch) over sides.
2 Beat butter and sifted icing sugar in a small bowl with an electric mixer until smooth. Stir in 1 cup of the sifted flour. Press mixture evenly over base of pan.
3 Bake base for 15 minutes or until browned lightly.
4 Meanwhile, whisk eggs, caster sugar, rind, juice and remaining flour in a medium bowl until combined. Pour egg mixture over hot base.
5 Bake slice for a further 20 minutes or until firm. Cool slice in pan on a wire rack before cutting into squares. Just before serving, dust with exra sifted icing sugar.

tips When buying lemons, look for those that are bright and heavy; they have more juice and flavour. This slice can be stored, covered, in the refrigerator for up to 3 days.

PASSIONFRUIT VANILLA SLICE

PREP + COOK TIME 45 MINUTES (+ COOLING & REFRIGERATION) **MAKES** 8

1 SHEET PUFF PASTRY
¼ CUP (55G) CASTER (SUPERFINE) SUGAR
¼ CUP (35G) CORNFLOUR (CORNSTARCH)
1½ TABLESPOONS CUSTARD POWDER
1¼ CUPS (310ML) MILK
30G (1 OUNCE) BUTTER
1 EGG YOLK
½ TEASPOON VANILLA EXTRACT
PASSIONFRUIT ICING
¾ CUP (120G) ICING (CONFECTIONERS') SUGAR
1 TABLESPOON PASSIONFRUIT PULP
1 TEASPOON WATER, APPROXIMATELY

1 Preheat oven to 240°C/475°F. Grease an 8cm x 26cm (3¼-inch x 10½-inch) bar cake pan; line base and long sides of pan with foil, extending the foil over sides.

2 Place pastry sheet on an oven tray. Bake for 15 minutes or until puffed; cool. Split pastry in half horizontally; remove and discard any uncooked pastry from the centre. Flatten pastry pieces gently with your hand; trim both pieces to fit the pan. Place top half in pan, top-side down.

3 Meanwhile, combine sugar, cornflour and custard powder in a medium saucepan; gradually stir in milk, stirring over heat until mixture boils and thickens. Reduce heat; simmer, stirring, for 3 minutes or until custard is thick and smooth. Remove from heat; stir in butter, egg yolk and extract.

4 Spread hot custard over pastry in pan; top with remaining pastry, bottom-side up, pressing down gently. Cool to room temperature.

5 Meanwhile, make passionfruit icing.

6 Spread icing on pastry; leave to set at room temperature. Refrigerate 3 hours before cutting into pieces.

passionfruit icing Sift icing sugar into a small heatproof bowl; stir in passionfruit and enough water to make a thick paste. Place bowl over a small saucepan of simmering water; stir until icing is spreadable.

CHOC BROWNIES WITH SOUR CREAM FROSTING

PREP + COOK TIME 55 MINUTES (+ COOLING & REFRIGERATION) **MAKES** 16

125G (4 OUNCES) BUTTER, CHOPPED
185G (6 OUNCES) DARK (SEMI-SWEET) CHOCOLATE, CHOPPED
1 CUP (220G) CASTER (SUPERFINE) SUGAR
2 TEASPOONS VANILLA EXTRACT
2 EGGS, BEATEN LIGHTLY
1 CUP (150G) PLAIN (ALL-PURPOSE) FLOUR
½ CUP (60G) COARSELY CHOPPED PECANS

SOUR CREAM FROSTING

100G (3 OUNCES) DARK (SEMI-SWEET) CHOCOLATE, CHOPPED
¼ CUP (60G) SOUR CREAM

1 Preheat oven to 180°C/350°F. Grease a deep 19cm (8-inch) square cake pan; line base with baking paper.
2 Stir butter and chocolate in a small saucepan over low heat until melted. Transfer mixture to a large bowl; stir in sugar and extract, then eggs, sifted flour and nuts. Pour mixture into pan.
3 Bake brownie for 30 minutes or until set. Cool brownie in pan.
4 Make sour cream frosting.
5 Turn brownie out of pan; top with frosting. Refrigerate until set before cutting into pieces.

sour cream frosting Melt chocolate in a small heatproof bowl over a small saucepan of simmering water (make sure the water doesn't touch the base of the bowl). Add sour cream; stir constantly until mixture is smooth and glossy.

tip This brownie can be stored, covered, in the refrigerator for up to 4 days.

HONEY MUESLI BARS

PREP + COOK TIME 25 MINUTES (+ REFRIGERATION) **MAKES** 24

¼ CUP (35G) SESAME SEEDS
1 CUP (130G) TOASTED MUESLI
3 CUPS (105G) RICE BUBBLES
½ CUP (40G) DESICCATED COCONUT
¼ CUP (35G) SUNFLOWER SEEDS
125G (4 OUNCES) BUTTER, CHOPPED
⅓ CUP (115G) HONEY
⅓ CUP (95G) PEANUT BUTTER
½ CUP (110G) RAW SUGAR

1 Preheat oven to 180°C/350°F. Grease a 20cm x 30cm (8-inch x 12-inch) rectangular pan; line base and long sides with baking paper, extending the paper 5cm (2 inches) over sides.
2 Place sesame seeds on an oven tray; roast about 5 minutes or until toasted lightly.
3 Place toasted seeds in a large bowl with muesli, rice bubbles, coconut and sunflower seeds; stir until well combine.
4 Stir butter, honey, peanut butter and sugar in a small saucepan over medium heat, without boiling, until butter is melted and sugar is dissolved. Bring to the boil. Reduce heat; simmer, uncovered, without stirring, for 5 minutes. Pour over dry ingredients, stir to combine.
5 Press mixture firmly into pan. Cover; refrigerate until set before cutting into bars.
tip This slice can be stored, covered, in the refrigerator for up to 4 days.

APRICOT CHOC-CHIP MUESLI BARS

PREP + COOK TIME 1 HOUR (+ COOLING) MAKES 15

125G (4 OUNCES) BUTTER, CHOPPED
½ CUP (110G) FIRMLY PACKED BROWN SUGAR
2 TABLESPOONS HONEY
1½ CUPS (135G) ROLLED OATS
¼ CUP (40G) SUNFLOWER SEEDS
⅓ CUP (25G) DESICCATED COCONUT
½ TEASPOON GROUND CINNAMON
½ CUP (75G) FINELY CHOPPED DRIED APRICOTS
2 TABLESPOONS DARK CHOC BITS

1 Preheat oven to 180°C/350°F. Grease a deep 20cm (8-inch) square cake pan; line base and sides with baking paper, extending the paper 5cm (2 inches) over edges.

2 Stir butter, sugar and honey in a medium saucepan over low heat until sugar is dissolved. Stir in oats, sunflower seeds, coconut, cinnamon and apricots. Press mixture into pan.

3 Bake slice for 30 minutes or until firm to touch. Sprinkle with choc bits; bake a further 5 minutes. Mark into 15 bars while warm; cool in pan. Cut when cold.

tip This slice can be stored in an airtight container for up to 1 week.

FL OZ
REG'D.

WAFFLES WITH MAPLE SYRUP

PREP + COOK TIME 30 MINUTES **MAKES** 10

1¾ CUPS (260G) PLAIN (ALL-PURPOSE) FLOUR
¼ CUP (35G) SELF-RAISING FLOUR
¼ CUP (55G) CASTER (SUPERFINE) SUGAR
2 EGGS, SEPARATED
1½ CUPS (375ML) MILK
60G (2 OUNCES) BUTTER, MELTED
2 TABLESPOONS WATER
2 TABLESPOONS ICING (CONFECTIONERS') SUGAR
5 SCOOPS VANILLA ICE-CREAM
½ CUP (125ML) MAPLE SYRUP

1 Sift flours and caster sugar into a small bowl; make a well in the centre. Gradually stir in combined egg yolks and milk, then butter and the water until smooth.

2 Beat egg whites in a small bowl with an electric mixer until soft peaks form. Fold into mixture, in two batches.

3 Drop ⅓ cup of mixture onto a lightly greased, preheated waffle iron. Close iron; cook, 2 minutes or until golden brown. Repeat with remaining mixture.

4 Serve waffles topped with ice-cream and drizzled with syrup.

tips You will need a waffle iron for this recipe; they are available from kitchenware and some department stores. Make sure you use pure maple syrup and not maple-flavoured syrup; maple-flavoured syrup is made from sugarcane and is not an adequate substitute for the real thing. For other waffle topping ideas, see pages 234 & 235.

CHOCOLATE & HAZELNUTS

SERVE WAFFLES FROM PAGE 233 TOPPED WITH A SCOOP OF VANILLA ICE-CREAM, CHOCOLATE SAUCE AND CHOPPED ROASTED HAZELNUTS. DUST WITH SIFTED ICING (CONFECTIONERS') SUGAR.

BLUEBERRY & WALNUTS

SERVE WAFFLES FROM PAGE 233 TOPPED WITH A SCOOP OF VANILLA ICE-CREAM, WARMED BLUEBERRY JAM, FRESH BLUEBERRIES AND CHOPPED TOASTED WALNUTS. DUST WITH SIFTED ICING (CONFECTIONERS') SUGAR.

BANANA, PECAN & CARAMEL

SERVE WAFFLES FROM PAGE 233 TOPPED WITH A SCOOP OF VANILLA ICE-CREAM, SLICED BANANA, CARAMEL SAUCE AND CHOPPED ROASTED PECANS. DUST WITH SIFTED ICING (CONFECTIONERS') SUGAR.

Waffle TOPPINGS

STRAWBERRIES & ICE-CREAM

SERVE WAFFLES FROM PAGE 233 TOPPED WITH A SCOOP OF VANILLA ICE-CREAM, STRAWBERRY TOPPING AND HALVED FRESH STRAWBERRIES. DUST WITH SIFTED ICING (CONFECTIONERS') SUGAR.

ORANGE & WHITE CHOCOLATE PETIT FOURS

PREP + COOK TIME 55 MINUTES (+ STANDING) **MAKES** 28

180G (5½ OUNCES) BUTTER, SOFTENED
¾ CUP (165G) CASTER (SUPERFINE) SUGAR
3 TEASPOONS FINELY GRATED ORANGE RIND
3 EGGS
½ CUP (125ML) ORANGE JUICE
1½ CUPS (225G) SELF-RAISING FLOUR
2 TABLESPOONS PLAIN (ALL-PURPOSE) FLOUR
2 X 5CM (2-INCH) STRIPS ORANGE RIND
½ CUP (125ML) BOILING WATER

WHITE CHOCOLATE GANACHE

½ CUP (125ML) POURING CREAM
180G (5½ OUNCES) WHITE CHOCOLATE, CHOPPED FINELY

1 Preheat oven to 180°C/350°F. Grease a 20cm x 30cm (8-inch x 12-inch) rectangular pan; line base and long sides with baking paper, extending the paper 5cm (2 inches) over sides.

2 Beat butter, sugar and grated rind in a small bowl with an electric mixer until light and fluffy. Beat in eggs, one at a time. Stir in juice and sifted flours. Spread mixture into pan.

3 Bake cake about 35 minutes. Leave cake in pan for 10 minutes before transferring onto a wire rack to cool.

4 Meanwhile, make white chocolate ganache.

5 Slice rind into long thin strips; place in a small bowl with the boiling water. Soak 30 seconds; drain. Transfer rind to a small bowl of iced water; drain.

6 Using a 3.5cm (1½-inch) cutter, cut 28 rounds from cooled cake. Discard excess cake. Place cake rounds on a wire rack over a baking-paper-lined tray. Spread ganache on cakes; top with rind. Stand until set.

white chocolate ganache Bring cream to the boil in a small saucepan. Pour hot cream over chocolate in a small heatproof bowl; stir until smooth. Stand for 20 minutes or until thickened.

tips You can serve these petit fours in paper patty cases if you like. You could use candied orange peel instead of the thinly sliced orange rind. Petit fours are best made on the day of serving.

MUFFINS & SCONES

WHITE CHOC-CHIP & ORANGE MINI MUFFINS

PREP + COOK TIME 40 MINUTES **MAKES** 48

2 CUPS (300G) SELF-RAISING FLOUR
½ CUP (110G) CASTER (SUPERFINE) SUGAR
¾ CUP (135G) WHITE CHOC BITS
60G (2 OUNCES) BUTTER, MELTED
¾ CUP (180ML) MILK
1 EGG, BEATEN LIGHTLY
2 TEASPOONS FINELY GRATED ORANGE RIND
¼ CUP (60ML) ORANGE JUICE

GLACÉ ICING

1½ CUPS (240G) ICING (CONFECTIONERS') SUGAR
½ TEASPOON VEGETABLE OIL
2 TABLESPOONS WATER, APPROXIMATELY
PINK, BLUE, GREEN AND YELLOW FOOD COLOURING

1 Preheat oven to 200°C/400°F. Line four 12-hole (1-tablespoon/20ml) mini muffin pans with paper cases.
2 Sift flour and sugar into a medium bowl; stir in remaining ingredients. Do not over-mix; mixture should be lumpy. Spoon mixture into paper cases.
3 Bake muffins about 10 minutes. Leave muffins in pans for 2 minutes before turning, top-side up, onto wire racks to cool.
4 Meanwhile, make glacé icing.
5 Spread icing on cold muffins.

glacé icing Sift icing sugar into a small heatproof bowl; stir in oil and enough water to make a paste. Place bowl over a small saucepan of simmering water; stir icing until spreadable. Divide icing evenly into four small bowls; tint each icing with one of the four food colourings.

tip These muffins are best made on the day of serving. Uniced muffins can be frozen for up to 3 months.

ROCK CAKES

PREP + COOK TIME 30 MINUTES MAKES 18

2 CUPS (300G) SELF-RAISING FLOUR
¼ TEASPOON GROUND CINNAMON
⅓ CUP (75G) CASTER (SUPERFINE) SUGAR
90G (3 OUNCES) BUTTER, CHOPPED
1 CUP (160G) SULTANAS
1 EGG
½ CUP (125ML) MILK
1 TABLESPOON CASTER (SUPERFINE) SUGAR, EXTRA

1 Preheat oven to 200°C/400°F. Grease oven trays.
2 Sift flour, cinnamon and sugar into a medium bowl; rub in butter with your fingertips. Stir in sultanas, egg and milk. Do not over mix.
3 Drop rounded tablespoons of mixture onto trays about 5cm (2 inches) apart; sprinkle with extra sugar.
4 Bake cakes about 15 minutes. Cool on trays.

tips Rock cakes are not scones, but they are related. Be careful not to overcook rock cakes as they will firm up as they cool. When they look brown and firmish, give one a gentle push and, if it slides on the oven tray, they're all done.

MIXED BERRY MUFFINS

PREP + COOK TIME 30 MINUTES **MAKES** 12

2½ CUPS (375G) SELF-RAISING FLOUR
100G (3 OUNCES) BUTTER, CHOPPED COARSELY
1 CUP (220G) CASTER (SUPERFINE) SUGAR
1¼ CUPS (310ML) BUTTERMILK
1 EGG, BEATEN LIGHTLY
1⅓ CUPS (200G) FROZEN MIXED BERRIES

1 Preheat oven to 200°C/400°F. Line a 12-hole (⅓-cup/80ml) muffin pan with paper cases.
2 Sift flour into a large bowl; rub in butter. Stir in sugar, buttermilk and egg. Do not over-mix; mixture should be lumpy. Stir in berries. Spoon mixture into pan holes.
3 Bake muffins about 20 minutes. Leave muffins in pan for 5 minutes before turning, top-side up, onto a wire rack to cool. Dust with sifted icing (confectioners') sugar, if you like.

tips This recipe works well with any frozen or fresh berries. These muffins can be stored in an airtight container for up to 2 days.

variation

mango buttermilk muffins Omit the berries and replace with 1 small (300g) finely chopped mango.

BASIC SCONES

PREP + COOK TIME 50 MINUTES **MAKES** 9

2½ CUPS (375G) SELF-RAISING FLOUR
1 TABLESPOON CASTER (SUPERFINE) SUGAR
¼ TEASPOON SALT
30G (1 OUNCE) BUTTER, SOFTENED
¾ CUP (180ML) MILK
½ CUP (125ML) WATER, APPROXIMATELY

1 Preheat oven to 220°C/425°F. Grease a deep 19cm (8-inch) square cake pan.
2 Sift flour, sugar and salt into a large bowl; rub in butter with your fingertips. Make a well in centre of flour mixture; add milk and almost all of the water. Use a knife to cut the liquid through the flour mixture, into a soft, sticky dough. Add remaining water if needed. Knead dough on a floured surface until smooth.
3 Press dough out evenly to a 2cm (¾-inch) thickness. Using a 6cm (2½-inch) cutter, cut as many rounds as you can from dough. Place scones, just touching, in pan.
4 Gently knead scraps of dough together. Cut out more rounds; place in pan. Brush scones with a little extra milk.
5 Bake scones for 20 minutes or until browned and scones sound hollow when tapped firmly on the top with your fingers.

tip These scones can be stored in an airtight container for up to 2 days.

variation

date scones When making the basic scone mixture, stir ¾ cup (120g) finely chopped seeded dried dates into the flour mixture after the butter has been rubbed in. Replace the milk and water with 1¼ cups (310ml) buttermilk.

PUMPKIN SCONES

PREP + COOK TIME 35 MINUTES **MAKES** 16

40G (1½ OUNCES) BUTTER, SOFTENED
¼ CUP (55G) CASTER (SUPERFINE) SUGAR
1 EGG, BEATEN LIGHTLY
¾ CUP COOKED MASHED PUMPKIN
2½ CUPS (375G) SELF-RAISING FLOUR
½ TEASPOON GROUND NUTMEG
⅓ CUP (80ML) MILK, APPROXIMATELY

1 Preheat oven to 220°C/425°F. Grease two 20cm (8-inch) round sandwich pans.

2 Beat butter and sugar in a small bowl with an electric mixer until light and fluffy; beat in egg. Transfer mixture to a large bowl; stir in pumpkin, then sifted dry ingredients and enough milk to make a soft sticky dough.

3 Knead dough on a floured surface until smooth. Press dough out evenly until 2cm (¾-inch) thick. Using a 5cm (2-inch) cutter, cut as many rounds as you can from dough. Place rounds, just touching, in pans.

4 Gently knead scraps of dough together. Cut out more rounds; place in pans. Brush scones with a little extra milk.

5 Bake scones for 15 minutes or until browned and scones sound hollow when tapped firmly on the top with your fingers.

tip These scones can be stored in an airtight container for up to 2 days.

SULTANA
& LEMON SCONES

PREP + COOK TIME 35 MINUTES MAKES 16

2½ CUPS (375G) SELF-RAISING FLOUR
1 TABLESPOON CASTER (SUPERFINE) SUGAR
¼ TEASPOON SALT
30G (1 OUNCE) BUTTER
½ CUP (80G) SULTANAS
2 TEASPOONS GRATED LEMON RIND
¾ CUP (180ML) MILK
½ CUP (125ML) WATER, APPROXIMATELY

1 Preheat oven to 240°C/475°F. Grease a deep 19cm (8-inch) square cake pan.
2 Place flour, sugar and salt in a large bowl; rub in butter with your fingertips. Stir in sultanas and the rind.
3 Make a well in the centre of the flour mixture; add milk and almost all of the water. Using a knife, cut the liquid through the flour mixture to a soft, sticky dough. Add the remaining water only if needed. Knead dough quickly and lightly on a floured surface until smooth.
4 Press dough out evenly to a 2cm (¾-inch) thickness. Dip a 4.5cm (1¾-inch) round cutter into flour; cut as many rounds as you can from dough. Place scones, just touching, in pan.
5 Gently knead scraps of dough together. Cut out more rounds; place in pans. Brush scones with a little extra milk.
6 Bake scones for 15 minutes or until browned and scones sound hollow when tapped firmly on the top with your fingers. Serve warm or cooled.
tip These scones can be stored in an airtight container for up to 2 days.

BUTTERMILK SCONES

PREP + COOK TIME 35 MINUTES **MAKES** 16

2½ CUPS (375G) SELF-RAISING FLOUR
1 TABLESPOON CASTER (SUPERFINE) SUGAR
¼ TEASPOON SALT
30G (1 OUNCE) BUTTER, CHOPPED
1¼ CUPS (310ML) BUTTERMILK, APPROXIMATELY
STRAWBERRY JAM AND CREAM, TO SERVE

1 Preheat oven to 240°C/475°F. Grease a deep 19cm (8-inch) square cake pan.

2 Place flour, sugar and salt in a large bowl; rub in butter with your fingertips. Make a well in centre of flour mixture; add buttermilk. Using a knife, cut the buttermilk through the flour mixture to a soft, sticky dough. Knead dough quickly and lightly on a floured surface until smooth.

3 Press dough out evenly to a 2cm (¾-inch) thickness. Dip a 4.5cm (1¾-inch) round cutter into flour; cut as many rounds as you can from dough. Place scones, just touching, in pan.

4 Gently knead scraps of dough together. Cut out more rounds; place, just touching, in pan. Brush scones with a little milk.

5 Bake scones for 15 minutes or until browned and scones sound hollow when tapped firmly on the top with your fingers. Serve scones warm or cooled with jam and cream.

CRUNCHY
RASPBERRY MUFFINS

PREP + COOK TIME 35 MINUTES **MAKES** 10

2 CUPS (300G) SELF-RAISING FLOUR
½ TEASPOON GROUND CINNAMON
⅓ CUP (75G) CASTER (SUPERFINE) SUGAR
1 EGG, BEATEN LIGHTLY
60G (2 OUNCES) BUTTER, MELTED
1 CUP (250ML) BUTTERMILK
200G (6½ OUNCES) FRESH OR FROZEN RASPBERRIES

CRUNCHY NUT TOPPING

2 TABLESPOONS CASTER (SUPERFINE) SUGAR
⅓ CUP (40G) FINELY CHOPPED WALNUTS OR PECANS
¼ TEASPOON GROUND CINNAMON
¼ TEASPOON GROUND NUTMEG

1 Preheat oven to 200°C/400°F. Grease 10 holes of a 12-hole (⅓-cup/80ml) muffin pan.
2 Make crunchy nut topping.
3 Sift flour, cinnamon and sugar into a large bowl. Stir in combined egg, butter and buttermilk, then raspberries until just combined; do not over-mix, mixture should be lumpy. Spoon mixture into pan holes; sprinkle with topping.
4 Bake muffins about 20 minutes. Leave muffins in pan for 5 minutes before turning, top-side up, onto a wire rack to cool. Serve warm or cooled.
crunchy nut topping Combine ingredients in a small bowl.

BANANA DATE MUFFINS

PREP + COOK TIME 35 MINUTES **MAKES** 12

2 CUPS (300G) SELF-RAISING FLOUR
1 TEASPOON MIXED SPICE
½ CUP (110G) FIRMLY PACKED BROWN SUGAR
1 CUP (300G) MASHED BANANA
1 CUP (160G) COARSELY CHOPPED SEEDED DATES
3 EGGS, BEATEN LIGHTLY
⅓ CUP (80ML) VEGETABLE OIL
⅓ CUP (80ML) BUTTERMILK

1 Preheat oven to 200°C/400°F. Grease a 12-hole (⅓-cup/80ml) muffin pan.
2 Stir ingredients in a large bowl until just combined; do not over-mix. Spoon mixture into pan holes.
3 Bake muffins about 20 minutes. Leave muffins in pan for 5 minutes before turning, top-side up, onto a wire rack to cool. Serve warm or cooled.

tips You will need 2 large overripe bananas (460g) for the mashed banana required in this recipe. These muffins can be stored in an airtight container for up to 2 days.

BLUEBERRY MUFFINS

PREP + COOK TIME 35 MINUTES **MAKES** 6

2 CUPS (300G) SELF-RAISING FLOUR
¾ CUP (165G) FIRMLY PACKED BROWN SUGAR
1 CUP (150G) FRESH OR FROZEN BLUEBERRIES
1 EGG, BEATEN LIGHTLY
¾ CUP (180ML) BUTTERMILK
½ CUP (125ML) VEGETABLE OIL

1 Preheat oven to 200°C/400°F. Grease a 6-hole (¾-cup/180ml) texas muffin pan.
2 Place ingredients in a large bowl; stir until just combined. Do not over-mix; mixture should be lumpy. Spoon mixture into pan holes.
3 Bake muffins about 20 minutes. Leave muffins in pan for 5 minutes before turning, top-side up, onto a wire rack to cool. Serve warm or cooled.

tips If using frozen blueberries, use them unthawed to minimise their colour bleeding into the muffin mixture. These muffins can be stored in an airtight container for up to 2 days.

APPLE SPICE MUFFINS

PREP + COOK TIME 40 MINUTES **MAKES** 6

2 CUPS (300G) SELF-RAISING FLOUR
½ TEASPOON BICARBONATE OF SODA (BAKING SODA)
½ TEASPOON GROUND CINNAMON
1 TEASPOON GROUND GINGER
¼ TEASPOON GROUND NUTMEG
PINCH GROUND CLOVES
¼ CUP (55G) FIRMLY PACKED BROWN SUGAR
½ X 410G (13 OUNCES) CANNED PIE APPLES
1 EGG, BEATEN LIGHTLY
¾ CUP (180ML) MILK
60G (2 OUNCES) BUTTER, MELTED
1 SMALL APPLE (130G)
20G (¾ OUNCE) BUTTER, MELTED, EXTRA
2 TABLESPOONS CINNAMON SUGAR

1 Preheat oven to 200°C/400°F. Grease a 6-hole (¾-cup/180ml) texas muffin pan.

2 Sift flour, soda, spices and brown sugar into a large bowl. Stir in pie apples, then egg, milk and butter; mix until just combined. Spoon mixture into pan holes.

3 Peel, core and halve apple; slice each half thinly. Place an apple slice on top of each muffin; brush with extra butter, sprinkle with cinnamon sugar.

4 Bake muffins about 25 minutes. Leave muffins in pan for 5 minutes before turning, top-side up, onto a wire rack to cool. Serve warm or cooled.

tips Cinnamon sugar is available in the spice section of most supermarkets. These muffins can be stored in an airtight container for up to 2 days.

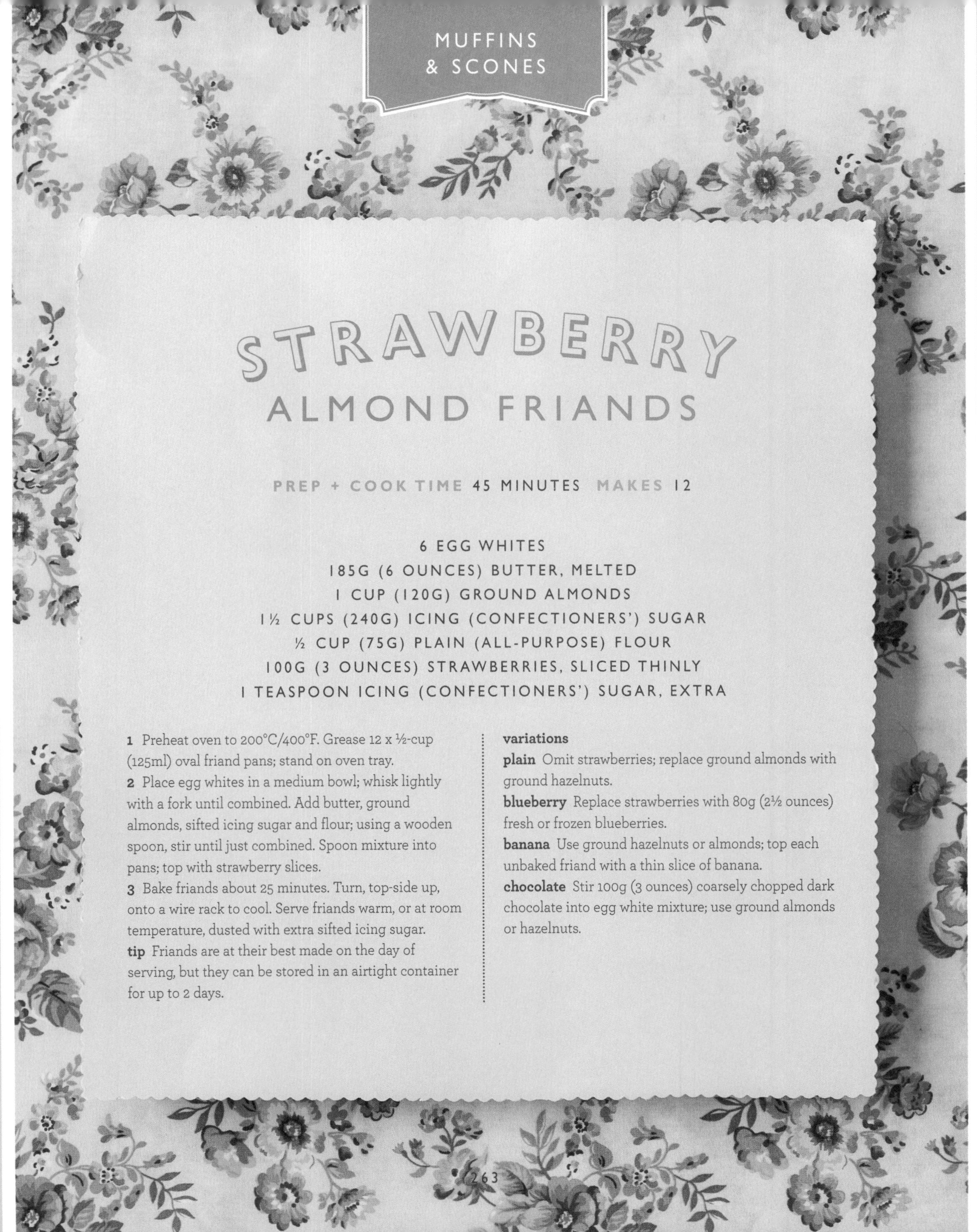

STRAWBERRY ALMOND FRIANDS

PREP + COOK TIME 45 MINUTES **MAKES** 12

6 EGG WHITES
185G (6 OUNCES) BUTTER, MELTED
1 CUP (120G) GROUND ALMONDS
1½ CUPS (240G) ICING (CONFECTIONERS') SUGAR
½ CUP (75G) PLAIN (ALL-PURPOSE) FLOUR
100G (3 OUNCES) STRAWBERRIES, SLICED THINLY
1 TEASPOON ICING (CONFECTIONERS') SUGAR, EXTRA

1 Preheat oven to 200°C/400°F. Grease 12 x ½-cup (125ml) oval friand pans; stand on oven tray.
2 Place egg whites in a medium bowl; whisk lightly with a fork until combined. Add butter, ground almonds, sifted icing sugar and flour; using a wooden spoon, stir until just combined. Spoon mixture into pans; top with strawberry slices.
3 Bake friands about 25 minutes. Turn, top-side up, onto a wire rack to cool. Serve friands warm, or at room temperature, dusted with extra sifted icing sugar.
tip Friends are at their best made on the day of serving, but they can be stored in an airtight container for up to 2 days.

variations
plain Omit strawberries; replace ground almonds with ground hazelnuts.
blueberry Replace strawberries with 80g (2½ ounces) fresh or frozen blueberries.
banana Use ground hazelnuts or almonds; top each unbaked friand with a thin slice of banana.
chocolate Stir 100g (3 ounces) coarsely chopped dark chocolate into egg white mixture; use ground almonds or hazelnuts.

RASPBERRY & WHITE CHOC FRIANDS

PREP + COOK TIME 45 MINUTES **MAKES** 8

6 EGG WHITES
185G (6 OUNCES) BUTTER, MELTED
1 CUP (120G) GROUND ALMONDS
1½ CUPS (240G) ICING (CONFECTIONERS') SUGAR
½ CUP (75G) PLAIN (ALL-PURPOSE) FLOUR
100G (3 OUNCES) COARSELY CHOPPED WHITE CHOCOLATE
100G (3 OUNCES) FRESH OR FROZEN RASPBERRIES
1 TEASPOON ICING (CONFECTIONERS') SUGAR, EXTRA

1 Preheat oven to 180°C/350°F. Grease 8 x ½-cup (125ml) rectangular friand pans; stand on oven tray.
2 Place egg whites in a medium bowl; whisk lightly with a fork until combined. Add butter, ground almonds, sifted icing sugar and flour, and chocolate; using a wooden spoon, stir until just combined. Spoon mixture into pans.
3 Bake friands 10 minutes. Top with raspberries; bake a further 15 minutes. Turn, top-side up, onto a wire rack to cool. Serve warm, or at room temperature, dusted with extra sifted icing sugar.

tips If using frozen berries, use them unthawed to minimise their colour bleeding into the friand mixture. Friands are at their best made on the day of serving, but they can be stored in an airtight container for 2 days, or frozen for up to 3 months. Frozen friands can be thawed, individually wrapped in foil, in a 180°C/350°F oven for about 15 minutes or in a microwave oven, wrapped in plastic wrap, on HIGH (100%) for about 30 seconds.

LEMON & POPPY SEED FRIANDS

PREP + COOK TIME 45 MINUTES **MAKES** 12

6 EGG WHITES
2 TEASPOONS FINELY GRATED LEMON RIND
1 TABLESPOON POPPY SEEDS
185G (6 OUNCES) BUTTER, MELTED
1 CUP (120G) GROUND ALMONDS
1½ CUPS (240G) ICING (CONFECTIONERS') SUGAR
½ CUP (75G) PLAIN (ALL-PURPOSE) FLOUR
1 TEASPOON ICING (CONFECTIONERS') SUGAR, EXTRA

1 Preheat oven to 200°C/400°F. Grease 12 x ½-cup (125ml) oval friand pans or a 12-hole (⅓-cup/80ml) muffin pan; stand on oven tray.
2 Place egg whites in medium bowl; whisk lightly with a fork until combined. Add rind, seeds, butter, ground almonds, sifted icing sugar and flour; using a wooden spoon, stir until just combined. Spoon mixture into pans.
3 Bake friands about 25 minutes. Turn, top-side up, onto wire rack to cool. Serve friands warm, or at room temperature, dusted with extra sifted icing sugar.

tips You could use orange rind instead of the lemon, or a mix of both. Friends are at their best made on the day of serving, but can be stored in an airtight container for 2 days, or frozen for up to 3 months. Frozen friands can be thawed, individually wrapped in foil, in a 180°C/350°F oven for about 15 minutes or in a microwave oven, wrapped in plastic wrap, on HIGH (100%) for about 30 seconds.

CHERRY FRIANDS

PREP + COOK TIME 45 MINUTES MAKES 12

6 EGG WHITES
185G (6 OUNCES) BUTTER, MELTED
1 CUP (120G) GROUND ALMONDS
1½ CUPS (240G) ICING (CONFECTIONERS') SUGAR
½ CUP (75G) PLAIN (ALL-PURPOSE) FLOUR
250G (8 OUNCES) FRESH CHERRIES, HALVED, SEEDED
1 TEASPOON ICING (CONFECTIONERS') SUGAR, EXTRA

1 Preheat oven to 200°C/400°F. Grease 12 x ½-cup (125ml) rectangular friand pans or a 12-hole (⅓-cup/80ml) muffin pan; stand on oven tray.

2 Place egg whites in a medium bowl; whisk lightly with a fork until combined. Add butter, ground almonds, sifted icing sugar and flour; using a wooden spoon, stir until just combined. Spoon mixture into pans; top with cherries.

3 Bake friands about 25 minutes. Turn, top-side up, onto a wire rack to cool. Serve friands warm, or at room temperature, dusted with extra sifted icing sugar.

tips Fresh cherries can be frozen for up to 18 months. Freeze in 250g (8-ounce) batches. If using frozen cherries, use them unthawed to minimise their colour bleeding into the mixture. Friands are at their best made on the day of serving, but can be stored in an airtight container for 2 days, or frozen for up to 3 months.

Old-fashioned MILKSHAKES

CHOCOLATE MILKSHAKE

PREP TIME 5 MINUTES **SERVES** 1

BLEND 1 CUP (250ML) MILK, 1 SCOOP CHOCOLATE ICE-CREAM AND 2 TABLESPOONS RICH CHOCOLATE SAUCE UNTIL COMBINED. PLACE 2 SCOOPS CHOCOLATE ICE-CREAM INTO A GLASS; POUR MILKSHAKE OVER ICE-CREAM. TOP WITH WHIPPED CREAM, GRATED CHOCOLATE AND A MARASCHINO CHERRY.

STRAWBERRY MILKSHAKE

PREP TIME 5 MINUTES **SERVES** 1

BLEND 1 CUP (250ML) MILK, 1 SCOOP VANILLA ICE-CREAM, 4 FRESH HULLED STRAWBERRIES AND 1 TABLESPOON STRAWBERRY TOPPING UNTIL COMBINED. PLACE 2 SCOOPS VANILLA ICE-CREAM INTO A GLASS; POUR MILKSHAKE OVER ICE-CREAM. TOP WITH WHIPPED CREAM AND A FRESH STRAWBERRY.

VANILLA MILKSHAKE

PREP TIME 5 MINUTES **SERVES** 1

BLEND 1 CUP (250ML) MILK, 1 SCOOP VANILLA ICE-CREAM AND 1 TEASPOON VANILLA EXTRACT UNTIL COMBINED. PLACE 2 SCOOPS VANILLA ICE-CREAM INTO A GLASS; POUR MILKSHAKE OVER ICE-CREAM. TOP WITH WHIPPED CREAM, COLOURED SPRINKLES AND A MARASCHINO CHERRY.

CARAMEL MILKSHAKE

PREP TIME 5 MINUTES **SERVES** 1

BLEND 1 CUP (250ML) MILK, 1 SCOOP VANILLA ICE-CREAM AND 2 TABLESPOONS CANNED CARAMEL TOP 'N' FILL UNTIL COMBINED. PLACE 2 SCOOPS VANILLA ICE-CREAM INTO A GLASS; POUR MILKSHAKE OVER ICE-CREAM. TOP WITH WHIPPED CREAM AND CHOPPED PEANUTS.

BREADS & BUNS

C
A

PINK ICED FINGER BUNS

PREP + COOK TIME 45 MINUTES (+ STANDING & COOLING) MAKES 16

4 TEASPOONS (14G) DRY YEAST
¼ CUP (55G) CASTER (SUPERFINE) SUGAR
1½ CUPS (375ML) WARM MILK
4 CUPS (600G) PLAIN (ALL-PURPOSE) FLOUR
60G (2 OUNCES) BUTTER, CHOPPED
1 EGG, BEATEN LIGHTLY
½ CUP (80G) SULTANAS
¼ CUP (40G) DRIED CURRANTS
¼ CUP (20G) DESICCATED COCONUT

BUN GLAZE

1 TABLESPOON CASTER (SUPERFINE) SUGAR
1 TEASPOON POWDERED GELATINE
1 TABLESPOON HOT WATER

GLACÉ ICING

1 CUP (160G) ICING (CONFECTIONERS') SUGAR
10G (½ OUNCE) BUTTER, MELTED
1 TABLESPOON MILK, APPROXIMATELY
PINK FOOD COLOURING

1 Combine yeast, sugar and milk in a small bowl. Cover; stand in a warm place for 10 minutes or until frothy.
2 Sift flour into a large bowl; rub in butter. Stir in yeast mixture, egg and fruit; mix to a soft dough. Cover; stand in a warm place for 45 minutes or until doubled in size.
3 Preheat oven to 220°C/425°F. Grease two 20cm x 30cm (8-inch x 12-inch) rectangular pans.
4 Knead dough on a floured surface for 5 minutes or until smooth and elastic. Divide dough into 16 portions; shape into buns 15cm (6-inches) long. Place eight buns into each pan; cover loosely with lightly oiled plastic wrap. Stand in a warm place for 10 minutes or until buns are well risen.
5 Bake buns 8 minutes. Cover loosely with foil; bake a further 5 minutes or until golden brown.
6 Make bun glaze. Turn buns, top-side up, onto a wire rack; brush with hot glaze. Cool.
7 Make icing. Spread icing on cold buns; sprinkle with coconut.

bun glaze Stir ingredients in a small saucepan over low heat, without boiling, until sugar and gelatine have dissolved.

glacé icing Sift icing sugar into a small heatproof bowl, stir in butter and enough milk to make a firm paste; tint pink with colouring. Place bowl over a small saucepan of simmering water; stir until icing is spreadable.

HOT CROSS BUNS

PREP + COOK TIME 1 HOUR 35 MINUTES (+ STANDING & COOLING) **MAKES** 16

4 TEASPOONS (14G) DRIED YEAST
¼ CUP (55G) CASTER (SUPERFINE) SUGAR
1½ CUPS (375ML) WARM MILK
4 CUPS (600G) PLAIN (ALL-PURPOSE) FLOUR
1 TEASPOON MIXED SPICE
½ TEASPOON GROUND CINNAMON
60G (2 OUNCES) BUTTER
1 EGG
¾ CUP (120G) SULTANAS

FLOUR PASTE

½ CUP (75G) PLAIN (ALL-PURPOSE) FLOUR
2 TEASPOONS CASTER (SUPERFINE) SUGAR
⅓ CUP (80ML) WATER, APPROXIMATELY

GLAZE

1 TABLESPOON CASTER (SUPERFINE) SUGAR
1 TEASPOON GELATINE
1 TABLESPOON WATER

1 Whisk yeast, sugar and milk in a small bowl or jug until yeast dissolves. Cover; stand in a warm place about 10 minutes or until mixture is frothy.

2 Sift flour and spices into a large bowl; rub in butter. Stir in yeast mixture, egg and sultanas; mix to a soft, sticky dough. Cover; stand in a warm place for 45 minutes or until dough has doubled in size.

3 Grease a deep 22cm (9-inch) square cake pan.

4 Knead dough on a floured surface for 5 minutes or until smooth and elastic. Divide dough into 16 pieces; knead into balls. Place balls into pan, cover; stand in a warm place for 10 minutes or until buns have risen two-thirds of the way up the pan.

5 Preheat oven to 220°C/425°F.

6 Make flour paste for crosses; place in a piping bag fitted with a small plain tube. Pipe crosses on buns.

7 Bake buns for 30 minutes or until they sound hollow when tapped. Turn buns, top-side up, onto a wire rack.

8 Make glaze; brush hot glaze onto hot buns. Cool.

flour paste Combine flour and sugar in a cup. Gradually blend in enough of the water to form a smooth firm paste.

glaze Stir ingredients in a small saucepan over heat, without boiling, until sugar and gelatine are dissolved.

tips Hot cross buns are best made on the day of serving. Unglazed, the buns can be frozen for up to 3 months.

CINNAMON DOUGHNUTS

PREP + COOK TIME 2½ HOURS (+ STANDING) **MAKES** 18

3 TEASPOONS (10G) INSTANT YEAST
¼ CUP (60ML) LUKEWARM WATER
80G (2½ OUNCES) BUTTER
1 CUP (250ML) MILK
¼ CUP (55G) CASTER (SUPERFINE) SUGAR
½ TEASPOON SALT
2 EGG YOLKS
3 CUPS (450G) PLAIN (ALL-PURPOSE) FLOUR
CANOLA OIL, FOR DEEP-FRYING
1 CUP (220G) CASTER (SUPERFINE) SUGAR, EXTRA
2 TEASPOONS GROUND CINNAMON

1 Combine yeast and the water in a small bowl, stir until yeast is dissolved.
2 Place butter and milk in a small saucepan over high heat; stir until butter is melted. Cool until lukewarm.
3 Place yeast mixture, butter mixture, sugar, salt, egg yolks and sifted flour in a large bowl; beat with a wooden spoon until mixture forms a soft sticky dough. Cover bowl; stand in a warm place for about 1 hour or until dough has doubled in size.
4 Turn dough onto a lightly floured surface; knead gently until just smooth. Roll dough out until 1cm (½-inch) thick. Using a floured 8cm (3-inch) round cutter and a floured 2.5cm (1-inch) round cutter, cut rounds from dough, removing the centres with the smaller cutter. Repeat with remaining dough, re-rolling when necessary. Place rounds on baking-paper-lined oven trays. Stand for 15 minutes.
5 Heat oil in a large saucepan or wok until it reaches 150°C/300°F on a candy thermometer (or until the base of a wooden spoon bubbles when placed in the oil). Deep-fry doughnuts three at a time for 2 minutes each side or until golden brown. Drain on paper towel.
6 Toss doughnuts immediately in combined extra sugar and cinnamon; serve doughnuts warm. To create the doughnut toppings as pictured on pages 280 & 281, use the glazes below with your favourite sprinkles, crushed nuts and shredded coconut.

glazes

plain glaze Stir 2 cups (320g) sifted pure icing (confectioners') sugar and ¼ cup (60ml) lukewarm milk in a small bowl until combined. Dip the top half of the cooled doughnuts in icing; place on a wire rack to set.

coloured glaze Tint the plain glaze mixture with your favourite colour (or colours) of food colouring.

chocolate glaze Sift ¼ cup (25g) cocoa powder with the pure icing sugar when making the plain glaze mixture. Add a little more lukewarm milk if necessary.

tips Never walk away from hot oil; if doughnuts are over browning, reduce the heat of the oil. They are best eaten on the day of making. Reheat cold doughnuts in 10-second bursts in the microwave until just warm.

Doughnut TOPPINGS

BASIC WHITE BREAD

PREP + COOK TIME 1¼ HOURS (+ STANDING) **MAKES** 18 SLICES

3 TEASPOONS (10G) DRIED YEAST
2 TEASPOONS CASTER (SUPERFINE) SUGAR
⅔ CUP (160ML) WARM WATER
2½ CUPS (375G) PLAIN (ALL-PURPOSE) FLOUR
1 TEASPOON SALT
30G (1 OUNCE) BUTTER, MELTED
½ CUP (125ML) WARM MILK

1 Whisk yeast, sugar and the water in a small bowl until yeast dissolves. Cover; stand in a warm place for 10 minutes or until mixture is frothy.
2 Sift flour and salt into a large bowl; stir in butter, milk and yeast mixture to a soft dough. Knead dough on a floured surface for 10 minutes or until dough is smooth and elastic. Place dough into an oiled large bowl. Cover; stand in a warm place for 1 hour or until dough has doubled in size.
3 Preheat oven to 200°C/400°F. Oil a 10cm (4-inch) deep, 9cm x 15cm (3¼-inch x 6-inch) bread tin.
4 Knead dough on a floured surface until smooth. Divide dough in half. Roll each half into a ball; place side-by-side in bread tin. Dust with a little extra flour. Cover; stand in a warm place for 20 minutes or until dough has risen.
5 Bake bread for 45 minutes or until it sounds hollow when tapped. Turn onto a wire rack to cool.
tip Bread can be frozen sliced or as a whole loaf for up to 3 months.

COCONUT BANANA BREAD

PREP + COOK TIME 1 HOUR 40 MINUTES (+ STANDING) **SERVES** 10

1⅓ CUPS (200G) SELF-RAISING FLOUR
1 CUP (150G) PLAIN (ALL-PURPOSE) FLOUR
⅔ CUP (150G) FIRMLY PACKED BROWN SUGAR
½ CUP (40G) DESICCATED COCONUT
1½ CUPS MASHED BANANA
3 EGGS
⅔ CUP (160ML) VEGETABLE OIL
1 TEASPOON COCONUT ESSENCE
½ CUP (25G) FLAKED COCONUT

1 Preheat oven to 180°C/350°F. Grease a 14cm x 21cm (5½-inch x 8½-inch) loaf pan; line base and sides with baking paper, extending the paper 5cm (2 inches) over the sides.

2 Sift flours into a large bowl; stir in sugar, desiccated coconut and banana, then combined eggs, oil and essence until just combined. Spread mixture into pan; sprinkle flaked coconut on top, pressing down lightly.

3 Bake bread about 1 hour 20 minutes. Leave bread in pan for 10 minutes before turning, top-side up, onto a wire rack to cool.

tip You will need about 4 large overripe bananas (920g) for the amount of mashed banana required.

serving suggestion Serve bread toasted with butter.

FRUIT & NUT BUNS WITH CARAMEL ICING

PREP + COOK TIME 1 HOUR 20 MINUTES (+ STANDING) **MAKES** 12

2 TEASPOONS (7G) DRIED YEAST
1¼ CUPS (310ML) WARM MILK
¼ CUP (55G) FIRMLY PACKED BROWN SUGAR
1 CUP (150G) PLAIN (ALL-PURPOSE) FLOUR
100G (3 OUNCES) BUTTER, CHOPPED FINELY, SOFTENED
1 EGG
2 CUPS (300G) PLAIN (ALL-PURPOSE) FLOUR, EXTRA
1 TEASPOON SALT
2 TEASPOONS MIXED SPICE
½ CUP (80G) SULTANAS
½ CUP (95G) DARK CHOC BITS
½ CUP (80G) CHOPPED MIXED NUTS
1 EGG YOLK, BEATEN LIGHTLY

CARAMEL ICING

½ CUP (80G) ICING (CONFECTIONERS') SUGAR
1 TABLESPOON BROWN SUGAR
2 TEASPOONS BOILING WATER, APPROXIMATELY

1 Whisk yeast, milk and 2 teaspoons of the sugar in a large bowl until yeast dissolves; whisk in flour. Cover; stand in a warm place for 30 minutes or until frothy.
2 Stir butter, egg, remaining sugar and sifted extra flour, salt and spice into yeast mixture. Stir in sultanas, choc bits and nuts. Knead dough on a floured surface for 5 minutes or until smooth and elastic. Place dough in an oiled large bowl. Cover; stand in a warm place for 1½ hours or until dough has doubled in size.
3 Punch down dough; knead on a floured surface until smooth. Divide dough into 12 portions; shape each portion into 15cm (6-inch) long buns. Place on an oiled oven tray. Cover; stand in a warm place for 30 minutes or until doubled in size.
4 Preheat oven to 200°C/400°F.
5 Brush buns with egg yolk. Bake for 30 minutes or until buns sound hollow when tapped. Leave buns on tray for 5 minutes before transferring to a wire rack to cool.
6 Meanwhile, make caramel icing.
7 Drizzle icing onto cooled buns; stand until icing is set.

caramel icing Sift icing sugar into a small heatproof bowl; stir in brown sugar and the water until smooth and spreadable.

tip These buns are best made on the day of serving. Uniced buns can be frozen for up to 3 months.

GINGERBREAD LOAVES

PREP + COOK TIME 1 HOUR **MAKES** 16

200G (6½ OUNCES) BUTTER, SOFTENED
1¼ CUPS (275G) CASTER (SUPERFINE) SUGAR
¾ CUP (270G) TREACLE
2 EGGS
3 CUPS (450G) PLAIN (ALL-PURPOSE) FLOUR
1½ TABLESPOONS GROUND GINGER
3 TEASPOONS MIXED SPICE
1 TEASPOON BICARBONATE OF SODA (BAKING SODA)
¾ CUP (180ML) MILK

VANILLA ICING

3 CUPS (480G) ICING (CONFECTIONERS') SUGAR
2 TEASPOONS BUTTER, SOFTENED
½ TEASPOON VANILLA EXTRACT
⅓ CUP (80ML) MILK

1 Preheat oven to 180°C/350°F. Grease two 8-hole (½-cup/125ml) petite loaf pans.

2 Beat butter and sugar in a small bowl with an electric mixer until light and fluffy. Pour in treacle; beat 3 minutes. Beat in eggs, one at a time. Transfer mixture to a large bowl; stir in sifted dry ingredients, then milk. Spoon mixture into pan holes.

3 Bake loaves about 25 minutes. Leave loaves in pans for 5 minutes before turning, top-side up, onto wire racks to cool.

4 Meanwhile, make vanilla icing.

5 Spread icing on loaves; stand until set.

vanilla icing Sift icing sugar into a heatproof bowl; stir in butter, extract and milk to form a smooth paste. Place bowl over a small saucepan of simmering water; stir until icing is spreadable.

tip You could make this recipe in muffin pans; line holes of two 12-hole (⅓-cup/80ml) muffin pans with paper cases. Spoon mixture into cases. Bake for about 20 minutes.

300 mL
pop
COLA

A
C

CARAMEL APPLE PULL-APART

PREP + COOK TIME 50 MINUTES MAKES 12

2 CUPS (300G) SELF-RAISING FLOUR
30G (1 OUNCE) BUTTER, CHOPPED
1 CUP (250ML) MILK, APPROXIMATELY
⅓ CUP (65G) FIRMLY PACKED BROWN SUGAR
400G (12½ OUNCES) CANNED PIE APPLES
PINCH GROUND NUTMEG
½ TEASPOON GROUND CINNAMON
2 TABLESPOONS COARSELY CHOPPED ROASTED PECANS

CARAMEL TOPPING

¼ CUP (60ML) POURING CREAM
20G (¾ OUNCE) BUTTER
½ CUP (110G) FIRMLY PACKED BROWN SUGAR

1 Preheat oven to 200°C/400°F. Grease a deep 22cm (9-inch) round cake pan.

2 Sift flour into a medium bowl; rub in butter with your fingertips. Make a well in centre of flour mixture; stir in enough milk to mix to a soft, sticky dough. Knead dough on a floured surface until smooth.

3 Roll dough on floured baking paper into a 21cm x 40cm (8-inch x 16-inch) rectangle. Sprinkle dough with sugar, spread with combined apples and spices leaving a 3cm (1¼-inch) border around long edge. Using paper as a guide, roll dough up from long side like a swiss roll. Use a floured serrated knife to cut the roll into 12 slices. Place 11 slices upright around edge of pan; place remaining slice in centre.

4 Bake for 25 minutes or until golden brown in colour. Leave in pan for 5 minutes before turning, top-side up, onto a wire rack.

5 Meanwhile, make caramel topping.

6 Brush hot pull-apart evenly with hot caramel; sprinkle with nuts.

caramel topping Place ingredients in a small saucepan; stir constantly over heat, without boiling, until sugar is dissolved. Simmer, uncovered, without stirring, for 3 minutes or until mixture is thickened slightly.

CHELSEA BUNS

PREP + COOK TIME 1½ HOURS (+ STANDING) **MAKES** 12

4 TEASPOONS (14G) DRY YEAST
1 TEASPOON CASTER (SUPERFINE) SUGAR
3 CUPS (560G) PLAIN (ALL-PURPOSE) FLOUR
1½ CUPS (375ML) WARM MILK
½ TEASPOON GROUND CINNAMON
½ TEASPOON MIXED SPICE
¼ TEASPOON GROUND NUTMEG
2 TEASPOONS GRATED ORANGE RIND
1 TABLESPOON CASTER (SUPERFINE) SUGAR, EXTRA
1 EGG, BEATEN LIGHTLY
45G (1½ OUNCES) BUTTER, MELTED
15G (½ OUNCE) BUTTER, MELTED, EXTRA
2 TABLESPOONS RASPBERRY JAM
½ CUP (75G) DRIED CURRANTS
¼ CUP (55G) FIRMLY PACKED LIGHT BROWN SUGAR
½ CUP (60G) COARSELY CHOPPED TOASTED PECANS
3 TEASPOONS WARMED HONEY

COFFEE ICING

1½ CUPS (240G) ICING (CONFECTIONERS') SUGAR
15G (½ OUNCE) BUTTER, MELTED
2 TABLESPOONS WARM MILK
3 TEASPOONS INSTANT COFFEE GRANULES

1 Combine yeast, caster sugar, 1 tablespoon of the flour, and warm milk in a small bowl. Cover; stand in a warm place for 10 minutes or until frothy.

2 Combine remaining sifted flour, spices, rind and extra caster sugar in a large bowl, stir in egg, butter and yeast mixture; mix to a soft dough. Knead dough on floured surface for 10 minutes or until smooth and elastic. Place dough in large greased bowl. Cover; stand in a warm place about 1 hour or until doubled in size.

3 Grease two deep 22cm (9-inch) round cake pans.

4 Turn dough onto a floured surface; knead 1 minute. Roll dough into a 23cm x 36cm (9-inch x 14½-inch) rectangle. Brush dough with extra butter, spread with jam. Sprinkle with combined currants, brown sugar and nuts, leaving a 2cm (1-inch) border all around.

5 Roll dough up firmly from long side like a swiss roll. Cut dough evenly into 12 pieces; position six pieces, cut-side up, in each pan. Cover; stand in a warm place for 30 minutes or until risen slightly.

6 Meanwhile, preheat oven to 200°C/ 400°F.

7 Bake buns for 30 minutes or until golden brown.

8 Make coffee icing. Turn buns, top-side up, onto a wire rack. Brush hot buns with honey, drizzle with coffee icing; cool.

coffee icing Sift icing sugar into small bowl, stir in butter, milk and coffee until smooth.

SHEFFIELD
FIRTH

WHEATMEAL ROLLS

PREP + COOK TIME 45 MINUTES **MAKES** 12

1¼ CUPS (185G) WHITE SELF-RAISING FLOUR
1¼ CUPS (200G) WHOLEMEAL SELF-RAISING FLOUR
2 TEASPOONS WHITE (GRANULATED) SUGAR
1 TEASPOON SALT
60G (2 OUNCES) BUTTER, CHOPPED
¼ CUP (45G) COARSE WHEATMEAL
¾ CUP (180ML) MILK, APPROXIMATELY
1 EGG YOLK
1 TABLESPOON MILK, EXTRA

ROLL TOPPINGS

½ TEASPOON WHOLEMEAL PLAIN (ALL-PURPOSE) FLOUR
½ TEASPOON FINE SEA SALT
½ TEASPOON DRIED MIXED HERBS
½ TEASPOON POPPY SEEDS
½ TEASPOON SESAME SEEDS
½ TEASPOON CARAWAY SEEDS

1 Preheat oven to 200°C/400°F. Lightly grease two oven trays.

2 Sift flours, sugar and salt into a large bowl; rub in butter with your fingertips. Stir in wheatmeal and enough milk to make a soft dough. Knead dough on a floured surface until smooth.

3 Divide dough into 12 portions. Knead each portion until smooth. Place one roll in the centre of each tray, and position five rolls, almost touching, around the centre roll.

4 Brush rolls with combined egg yolk and extra milk. Sprinkle one roll on each tray with ¼ teaspoon of one of the roll toppings, not repeating a topping on the same tray; each batch of rolls should have all the different toppings.

5 Bake rolls for 20 minutes or until browned.

RICH DARK FRUIT LOAF

PREP + COOK TIME 2½ HOURS (+ STANDING) **SERVES** 12

1 CUP (160G) SULTANAS
½ CUP (75G) DRIED CURRANTS
¾ CUP (110G) COARSELY CHOPPED DRIED APRICOTS
1½ CUPS (250G) SEEDED DRIED DATES, HALVED
1 CUP (250ML) WARM WATER
2 TEASPOONS (7G) DRY YEAST
¼ CUP (60ML) WARM WATER, EXTRA
½ CUP (75G) WHITE PLAIN (ALL-PURPOSE) FLOUR
½ CUP (80G) WHOLEMEAL PLAIN (ALL-PURPOSE) FLOUR
1½ CUPS (225G) RYE FLOUR
2 TEASPOONS GROUND CINNAMON
½ TEASPOON GROUND CARDAMOM
½ TEASPOON GROUND CLOVES
½ TEASPOON GROUND NUTMEG
2 TEASPOONS POPPY SEEDS

1 Combine dried fruit and the water in a medium bowl. Cover; stand 30 minutes.

2 Combine yeast, extra water and 1 teaspoon of the white plain flour in a small bowl. Cover; stand in a warm place for 10 minutes or until frothy.

3 Sift remaining flours and spices into a large bowl; add husks left in the sifter to the mixture. Stir in undrained fruit mixture and yeast mixture; mix to a sticky dough. Knead dough on a floured surface for 5 minutes. Place dough in a large oiled bowl. Cover; stand in a warm place for 1 hour or until risen slightly.

4 Grease an oven tray. Knead dough on a floured surface for 5 minutes. Shape dough into a 15cm (6-inch) round, place on tray. Cover; stand in a warm place for 40 minutes or until risen slightly.

5 Meanwhile, preheat oven to 200°C/400°F.

6 Brush top of dough with water, then sprinkle with seeds; cover loosely with foil. Bake bread for 30 minutes; remove foil. Reduce oven to 180°C/350°F; bake a further 1¼ hours or until bread sounds hollow when tapped. (Cover bread loosely with foil if over-browning.) Turn bread, top-side up, onto a wire rack to cool.

TRADITIONAL DAMPER

PREP + COOK TIME 1 HOUR (+ STANDING) **SERVES** 10

3½ CUPS (525G) SELF-RAISING FLOUR
1 TEASPOON SALT
2 TEASPOONS CASTER (SUPERFINE) SUGAR
40G (1½ OUNCES) BUTTER
½ CUP (125ML) MILK
1¼ CUPS (310ML) WATER, APPROXIMATELY

1 Preheat oven to 200°C/400°F. Grease an oven tray.
2 Sift flour, salt and sugar into a large bowl; rub in butter with your fingertips. Stir in milk and enough water to mix to a sticky dough. Knead dough on a floured surface until just smooth.
3 Place dough on oven tray; press into a 16cm (6½-inch) round. Cut a cross into top of dough, about 1cm (½ inch) deep. Brush dough with a little extra milk; sprinkle with a little extra flour.
4 Bake damper about 45 minutes. Transfer, top-side up, onto a wire rack to cool.

tip Damper is an iconic Australian substitute for bread. It was created by the early settlers as they travelled west and fresh bread wasn't available.

serving suggestion Serve damper with butter and golden syrup.

IRISH
SODA BREAD

PREP + COOK TIME 1½ HOURS **SERVES** 8

2½ CUPS (375G) WHITE PLAIN (ALL-PURPOSE) FLOUR
2⅔ CUPS (420G) WHOLEMEAL PLAIN (ALL-PURPOSE) FLOUR
1 TEASPOON SALT
1 TEASPOON BICARBONATE OF SODA (BAKING SODA)
2¾ CUPS (680ML) BUTTERMILK, APPROXIMATELY

1 Preheat oven to 180°C/350°F. Grease an oven tray.
2 Sift flours, salt and soda into a large bowl; add any wholemeal husks from the sieve to the bowl. Stir in enough of the buttermilk to make a firm dough. Knead dough on a floured surface until just smooth.
3 Shape dough into a 20cm (8-inch) round; place on tray. Using a sharp knife, cut a cross into top of dough, about 1cm (½ inch) deep.
4 Bake bread about 50 minutes. Transfer, top-side up, onto a wire rack to cool.

serving suggestions Serve with butter and jam.

GLOSSARY

ALLSPICE also called pimento or jamaican pepper; so-named because it tastes like a combination of nutmeg, cumin, clove and cinnamon. Available whole or ground, and used in both sweet and savoury dishes.

ALMONDS flat, pointy-tipped nuts with a pitted brown shell enclosing a creamy white kernel which is covered by a brown skin.

BLANCHED brown skins removed.

ESSENCE made with almond oil and alcohol or another agent.

FLAKED paper-thin slices.

GROUND also called almond meal; nuts are powdered to a coarse flour-like texture.

SLIVERED small pieces cut lengthways.

VIENNA toffee-coated almonds.

ARROWROOT a starch made from the rhizome of a Central American plant, used mostly as a thickening agent. Cornflour can be substituted but does not make as clear a glaze and imparts its own taste.

BAGEL small ring-shaped bread roll; yeast-based but egg-less, with a dense, chewy texture and shiny crust. A true bagel is boiled in water before it's baked.

BAKE BLIND a cooking term to describe baking a pie shell or pastry case before filling is added. If a filling does not need to be baked or is very wet, you may need to "blind-bake" the unfilled shell. To bake blind, ease the pastry into a pan or dish, place on an oven tray; line the pastry with baking paper then fill with dried beans, uncooked rice or "baking beans" (also called pie weights). Bake according to the recipe's directions then cool before adding the suggested filling.

BAKING PAPER also called parchment paper or baking parchment – is a silicone-coated paper that is primarily used for lining baking pans and oven trays so cakes and biscuits won't stick, making removal easy.

BAKING POWDER a raising agent consisting mainly of two parts cream of tartar to one part bicarbonate of soda (baking soda). The acid and alkaline combination, when moistened and heated, gives off carbon dioxide which aerates and lightens a mixture during baking

BAMBOO SKEWERS used for cocktail-sized skewers and satay instead of metal skewers; should be soaked in water for 1 hour before use to help prevent splintering or scorching during cooking. Available in several different lengths.

BICARBONATE OF SODA (BAKING SODA) a raising agent.

BISCUITS also known as cookies; almost always an "eat-in-your-hand"-sized soft or crisp sweet cake.

BLOOD ORANGE a virtually seedless citrus fruit with blood-red-streaked rind and flesh; sweet, non-acidic, salmon-coloured pulp and juice having slight strawberry or raspberry overtones. The juice can be drunk straight or used in cocktails, sauces, sorbets and jellies; can be frozen for use in cooking when the growing season finishes. The rind is not as bitter as an ordinary orange.

BRIOCHE French in origin; a rich, yeast-leavened, cake-like bread made with butter and eggs. Available from cake or specialty bread shops.

BREADCRUMBS, STALE crumbs made by grating, blending or processing one- or two- day-old bread.

BUCKWHEAT a herb in the same plant family as rhubarb; not a cereal so it is gluten-free. Available as flour; ground (cracked) into coarse, medium or fine granules (kasha) and used similarly to polenta.

BUTTER we use salted butter unless stated otherwise; 125g is equal to 1 stick (4 ounces). Unsalted or "sweet" butter has no salt added and is perhaps the most popular butter among pastry-chefs.

BUTTERMILK originally the term given to the slightly sour liquid left after butter was churned from cream, today it is made from no-fat or low-fat milk to which specific bacterial cultures have been added. Despite its name, it is low in fat.

CACHOUS also known as dragées in some countries; minuscule (3mm to 5mm) metallic-looking-but-edible confectionery balls used in cake decorating; available in silver, gold or various colours.

CARAMEL TOP 'N' FILL see Milk

CARDAMOM a spice native to India and used extensively in its cuisine; can be purchased in pod, seed or ground form. Has a distinctive aromatic, sweetly rich flavour and is one of the world's most expensive spices. Used to flavour curries, rice dishes, sweet desserts and cakes.

CASHEWS plump, kidney-shaped, golden-brown nuts with a sweet, buttery flavour; contains about 48% fat. Because of this high fat content, they should be kept, sealed tightly, in the fridge to avoid becoming rancid. We use roasted unsalted cashews unless stated otherwise; they are available from healthfood stores and most supermarkets. Roasting cashews brings out their intense nutty flavour. See also Roasting/toasting

CHAMPAGNE we use sweet sparkling wine in this book rather than the more expensive French original.

CHEESE

COTTAGE fresh, white, unripened curd cheese with a lumpy consistency and mild, sweet flavour. Fat content ranges between 15 to 55%, determined by whether it is made from whole, low-fat or fat-free cow milk.

CREAM CHEESE commonly called philadelphia or philly; a soft cow's-milk cheese, its fat content ranges from 14 to 33%.

MASCARPONE an Italian fresh cultured-cream product made in much the same way as yoghurt. Whiteish to creamy yellow in colour, with a soft, creamy buttery-rich, luscious texture.

RICOTTA a soft, sweet, moist, white cow's-milk cheese with a low fat content (8.5%) and a slightly grainy texture. The name roughly translates as "cooked again" and refers to ricotta's manufacture from a whey that is itself a by-product of other cheese making.

CHERRIES small, soft stone fruit varying in colour from yellow to dark red. Sweet cherries are eaten whole and in desserts while sour cherries such as the morello variety are used for jams, preserves, pies and savoury dishes (particularly good with game birds and meats).

GLACÉ also known as candied cherries; boiled in heavy sugar syrup, and then dried.

MARASCHINO pronounced mahr-uh-skee-no. Any variety of cherry can be used; maraschino are macerated in a flavoured and coloured sugar syrup then preserved. Originally an Italian confection, these are most often found in cocktails or as a colourful garnish, but they can be used in baked items and fruit salads.

MORELLO sour cherries available bottled in syurp. Used in baking and savoury dishes and are a good match for game.

CHINESE FIVE-SPICE a fragrant mixture of ground cinnamon, cloves, star anise, sichuan pepper and fennel seeds.

CHOCOLATE

CHERRY RIPE dark chocolate bar made with coconut and cherries; standard size bar weighs 55g (2 ounces).

CHOC BITS also known as chocolate chips or chocolate morsels; available in milk, white and dark chocolate. Made of cocoa liquor, cocoa butter, sugar and an emulsifier, these hold their shape in baking and are ideal for decorating.

COUVERTURE a term used to describe a fine quality, very rich chocolate high in both cocoa butter and cocoa liquor. Requires tempering when used to coat but not if used in baking, mousses or fillings.

DARK (SEMI-SWEET) also called luxury chocolate; made of a high percentage of cocoa liquor and cocoa butter, and little added sugar. Dark chocolate is ideal for use in desserts and cakes.

MELTS small discs of compounded milk, white or dark chocolate ideal for melting and moulding.

MILK most popular eating chocolate, mild and very sweet; similar in make-up to dark with the difference being the addition of milk solids.

WHITE contains no cocoa solids but derives its sweet flavour from cocoa butter. Very sensitive to heat.

CHOCOLATE HAZELNUT SPREAD also known as Nutella; made of cocoa powder, hazelnuts, sugar and milk.

CINNAMON available in the piece (called sticks or quills) and ground into powder; one of the world's most common spices, used universally as a sweet, fragrant flavouring for both sweet and savoury foods. The dried inner bark of the shoots of the Sri Lankan native cinnamon tree; much of what is sold as the real thing is in fact cassia, Chinese cinnamon, from the bark of the cassia tree. Less expensive to process than true cinnamon, it is often blended with Sri Lankan cinnamon to produce the type of "cinnamon" most commonly found in supermarkets

CLOVES dried flower buds of a tropical tree; available whole or ground. Has a strong scent and taste so use sparingly.

COCOA POWDER also known as unsweetened cocoa; cocoa beans (cacao seeds) that have been fermented, roasted, shelled, ground into powder then cleared of most of the fat content. Unsweetened cocoa is used in hot chocolate drink mixtures; milk powder and sugar are added to the ground product.

DUTCH-PROCESSED is treated with an alkali to neutralise its acids. It has a reddish-brown colour, a mild flavour and is easy to dissolve.

COCONUT

CREAM obtained commercially from the first pressing of the coconut flesh alone, without the addition of water; the second pressing (less rich) is sold as coconut milk. Available in cans and cartons at supermarkets.

DESICCATED concentrated, dried, unsweetened and finely shredded coconut flesh.

ESSENCE synthetically produced from flavouring, oil and alcohol.

FLAKED dried flaked coconut flesh.

MILK not the liquid found inside the fruit (coconut water), but the diluted liquid from the second pressing of the white flesh of a mature coconut (the first pressing produces coconut cream). Available in cans and cartons at most supermarkets.

SHREDDED unsweetened thin strips of dried coconut flesh.

CORN FLAKES commercially manufactured cereal made of dehydrated then baked crisp flakes of corn. Also available is a prepared finely ground mixture used for coating or crumbing food before frying or baking, sold as "crushed corn flakes" in most supermarkets

CORN SYRUP a sweet syrup made by heating cornstarch under pressure. It comes in light and dark types and is used in baking and confectionery. It is sometimes mixed with other sugars such as honey.

CORNFLOUR (CORNSTARCH) available made from corn or wheat (wheaten cornflour, gluten-free, gives a lighter texture in cakes); used as a thickening agent in cooking.

CRANBERRIES available dried and frozen; have a rich, astringent flavour and can be used in cooking sweet and savoury dishes. The dried version can usually be substituted for or with other dried fruit.

CRANBERRY SAUCE a manufactured product made of cranberries cooked in sugar syrup; the astringent flavour goes beautifully with roast poultry and barbecued meats.

CREAM

POURING also known as pure or fresh cream. It has no additives and contains a minimum fat content of 35%.

SOUR a thick, commercially-cultured sour cream with a minimum fat content of 35%.

THICK (DOUBLE) a dolloping cream with a minimum fat content of 45%.

THICKENED (HEAVY) a whipping cream that contains a thickener. It has a minimum fat content of 35%.

CREAM OF TARTAR the acid ingredient in baking powder; added to confectionery mixtures to help prevent sugar from crystallising. Keeps frostings creamy and improves volume when beating egg whites.

CRÈME FRAÎCHE a mature, naturally fermented cream (minimum fat content 35%) having a velvety texture and slightly tangy, nutty flavour. Crème fraîche, a French variation of sour cream, can boil without curdling and be used in sweet and savoury dishes.

CUSTARD POWDER instant mixture used to make pouring custard; it is similar to North American instant pudding mixes.

DATES fruit of the date palm tree, eaten fresh or dried, on their own or in prepared dishes. About 4cm to 6cm in length, oval and plump, thin-kinned, with a honey-sweet flavour and sticky texture. Best known, perhaps, for their inclusion in sticky toffee pudding: also found in muesli; muffins, scones and cakes; compotes and stewed fruit desserts.

DOCKING PASTRY a docker has a spiked roller to prick holes in uncooked dough so that it will not puff up when baked. Alternatively, you can use a fork to prick the pastry all over.

DRIED CURRANTS dried tiny, almost black raisins so named from the grape type native to Corinth, Greece; most often used in jams, jellies and sauces (the best-known of which is the English cumberland sauce). These are not the same as fresh currants, which are the fruit of a plant in the gooseberry family.

EGGS we use large chicken eggs weighing an average of 60g (2 ounces). If a recipe calls for raw or barely cooked eggs, exercise caution if there is a salmonella problem in your area, particularly in food eaten by children and pregnant women. Shell colour is determined by the breed of hen and what it has been fed on; it has nothing to do with quality. As far as the differences between cage, barn-laid and free-range eggs is concerned, nutrient content, value for money and taste have all got to be factored into the equation; in the end, the decision is left to individual preference. Store eggs, in the carton they come in, under refrigeration as soon as you bring them home to slow down deterioration. This helps reduce water loss and protects them from absorbing flavour from other fridge items. Most eggs can be kept, in their carton, in the fridge, for up to 4 weeks.

EGGWASH beaten egg (white, yolk or both) and milk or water; often brushed over pastry or bread to impart colour or gloss.

ESSENCE/EXTRACT an essence is either a distilled concentration of a food quality or an artificial creation of it. Coconut and almond essences are synthetically produced substances used in small amounts to impart their respective flavours to foods. An extract is made by actually extracting the flavour from a food product. In the case of vanilla, pods are soaked, usually in alcohol, to capture the authentic flavour. Essences and extracts keep indefinitely if stored in a cool dark place.

FIGS are best eaten in peak season, at the height of summer. Vary in skin and flesh colour according to type not ripeness. When ripe, figs should be unblemished and bursting with flesh; nectar beads at the base indicate when a fig is best. Figs are also glacéd, dried or canned in sugar syrup.

FLOUR

BAKER'S also known as gluten-enriched, strong or bread-mix flour. Produced from a variety of what has a high gluten (protein) content and is best suited for pizza and bread making: the expansion caused by the yeast and the stretchiness imposed by kneading require a flour that is "strong" enough to handle these stresses. Since domestic breadmakers entered the marketplace, it has become easier to find strong flour; look for it at your supermarket or health-food store.

MAIZE milled from maize (corn); finely ground polenta (cornmeal) can be substituted in some instances.

PLAIN (ALL-PURPOSE) unbleached wheat flour; is the best for baking as the gluten content ensures a strong dough for a light result.

RICE very fine, almost powdery, gluten-free flour; made from ground white rice. Used in baking, as a thickener, and in some Asian noodles and desserts. Another variety, made from glutinous sweet rice, is used for chinese dumplings and rice paper.

RYE is greyish, with a pleasant sour tang and little gluten, and is usally mixed with wheat flour for breadmaking.

SELF-RAISING plain (all-purpose) white or wholemeal flour sifted with added baking powder; make at home in the proportion of 1 cup flour to 2 teaspoons baking powder.

SEMOLINA coarsely ground flour milled from durum wheat; the flour used in making gnocchi, pasta and couscous.

WHOLEMEAL also known as wholewheat flour; milled with the wheat germ so is higher in fibre and more nutritional than plain flour.

FOOD COLOURING vegetable-based substance available in liquid, paste or gel form.

FRIAND PAN traditional friand pans have oval-or rectangular-shaped holes; available separately or, in frames of various sizes. They are made in various materials with different finishes.

FROMAGE FRAIS a light, fresh French cheese that has the consistency of thick yoghurt with a refreshing, slightly tart taste. Low fat varieties are available.

FRUIT MINCE also known as mincemeat. A mixture of dried fruits such as raisins, sultanas and candied peel, nuts, spices, apple, brandy or rum. Is used as a filling for cakes, puddings and fruit mince pies.

GANACHE pronounced gah-nash; a creamy chocolate filling or frosting for cakes. Depending on its intended use, it is made from varying proportions of good-quality chocolate and pouring cream. Other ingredients can be added for flavour, or to increase its richness or gloss. Ganache can be whipped, piped or poured like a glaze, and can be frozen for up to 3 months.

GELATINE a thickening agent; we use dried (powdered) gelatine; it's also available in sheets known as leaf gelatine. Made from either collagen, a protein found in animal connective tissue and bones, or certain algae (agar-agar). Three teaspoons of dried gelatine (8g or one sachet) is about the same as four leaves. Professionals use leaf gelatine because it generally results in a smoother, clearer consistency; it is also most commonly used throughout Europe than elsewhere. The two types are interchangable but leaf gelatine gives a much clearer mixture than powdered gelatine; it's perfect in dishes where appearance really counts

GINGER

FRESH also called green or root ginger; the thick gnarled root of a tropical plant. Can be kept, peeled, covered with dry sherry in a jar and refrigerated, or frozen in an airtight container.

GLACÉ fresh ginger root preserved in sugar syrup; crystallised ginger can be used if rinsed with warm water and dried before using.

GROUND also called powdered ginger; used as a flavouring in baking but cannot be substituted for fresh ginger.

GLACÉ FRUIT fruit, such as peaches, pineapple and oranges, cooked in a heavy sugar syrup then dried.

GLUCOSE SYRUP also known as liquid glucose, made from wheat starch. Available at most supermarkets.

GLUTEN one of the proteins in wheat and most other cereal flours that helps act as a leavening agent. See also Flour

GOLDEN SYRUP a by-product of refined sugarcane; pure maple syrup or honey can be substituted. Golden syrup and treacle (a thicker, darker syrup not unlike molasses), also known as flavour syrups, are similar sugar products made by partly breaking down sugar into its component parts and adding water. Treacle is more viscous, and has a stronger flavour and aroma than golden syrup (which has been refined further and contains fewer impurities, so is lighter in colour and more fluid). Both can be use in baking and for making confectionery items.

GREASING/OILING PANS use butter or margarine (for sweet baking), oil or cooking-oil spray (for savoury baking) to grease baking pans; overgreasing pans can cause food to overbrown. Use paper towel or a pastry brush to spread the oil or butter over the pan. Try covering your hand with a small plastic bag then swiping it into the butter or margarine.

HAZELNUTS also known as filberts; plump, grape-sized, rich, sweet nut having a brown skin that is removed by rubbing heated nuts together vigorously in a tea-towel.

GROUND is made by grinding the hazelnuts to a coarse flour texture for use in baking or as a thickening agent.

HONEY the variety sold in a squeezable container is not suitable for the recipes in this book.

ICE-CREAM we use a good quality ice-cream having 5g of fat per 100ml for the recipes in this book.

JAM also known as preserve or conserve; a thickened mixture of a fruit (and occasionally, a vegetable) and sugar. Usually eaten on toast for breakfast, it's also used as a filling or icing for sweet biscuits and cakes.

KAFFIR LIME also known as magrood, leech lime or jeruk purut. The wrinkled, bumpy-skinned green fruit of a small citrus tree originally grown in South Africa and South East Asia. As a rule, only the rind and leaves are used.

KAFFIR LIME LEAVES also called bai magrood and looks like two glossy dark green leaves joined end to end, in a rounded hourglass shape. Used fresh or dried in many South-East Asian dishes, they are used like bay leaves or curry leaves. Sold fresh, dried or frozen, the dried leaves are less potent so double the number if using them as a substitute for fresh; a strip of fresh lime peel may be substituted for each kaffir lime leaf.

KITCHEN STRING made of a natural product such as cotton or hemp so that it neither affects the flavour of the food it's tied around nor melts when heated.

KIWIFRUIT also known as Chinese gooseberry; having a brown, somewhat hairy skin and bright-green flesh with a unique sweet-tart flavour. Used in fruit salads, desserts and eaten (peeled) as is.

LAMINGTON PAN this pan is straight-sided and measures 20cm x 30cm x 3cm (8 inches x 12 inches x 1¼ inches). It is used for making the cake which is then made into lamingtons; it's also used for slizes.

LIQUEURS

COINTREAU citrus-flavoured liqueur.

GRAND MARNIER orange liqueur based on cognac-brandy.

KAHLUA coffee-flavoured liqueur.

KIRSCH cherry-flavoured liqueur.

LIMONCELLO Italian lemon-flavoured liqueur; originally made from the juice and peel of lemons grown along the Amalfi coast.

RUM we use a dark underproof rum (not overproof) for a more subtle flavour in cooking. White rum is almost colourless, sweet and used mostly in mixed drinks.

TIA MARIA coffee-flavoured liqueur

MACADAMIAS native to Australia; fairly large, slightly soft, buttery rich nut. Should always be stored in the fridge to prevent their high oil content turning them rancid.

MANDARIN also known as tangerine; a small, loose-skinned, easy-to-peel, sweet and juicy citrus fruit, prized for its eating qualities more than for juicing. Segments in a light syrup are available canned.

MANDOLINE a hand-operated implement with adjustable blades for thick to very thin slicing, shredding, dicing and cutting into match- or straw-sized sticks with speed and precision; ideal for shredding carrot and making french fries. Similar results can be achieved with a food processor or V-slicer and, as a last resort, the coarse side of a grater. Caution is advised when hand-operating this extremely sharp instrument.

MANGO tropical fruit originally from India and South East Asia. With skin colour ranging from green to yellow and deep red; fragrant, deep yellow flesh surrounds a large flat seed. Halved, seeded, cross-hatched with a knife then turned inside out shows the sweet, luscious, juicy flesh at its best. Mangoes can also be used in curries, salsas and sambals, or pureed for ice-cream, mousse or smoothies. Mango cheeks in light syrup are available canned. Sour and crunchy, green mangoes are just immature fruit that can be eaten as a vegetable in salads, salsas, curries and stir-fries. They will keep, wrapped in plastic, in the fridge for up to 2 weeks.

MAPLE-FLAVOURED SYRUP is made from sugar cane and is also known as golden or pancake syrup. It is not a substitute for pure maple syrup.

MAPLE SYRUP (PURE) distilled from the sap of sugar maple trees. Maple-flavoured syrup or pancake syrup is not an adequate substitute for the real thing.

MARMALADE a preserve, usually based on citrus fruit and its rind, cooked with sugar until the mixture has an intense flavour and thick consistency. Orange, lemon and lime are some of the commercially prepared varieties available.

MARZIPAN made from ground almonds, sugar and glucose. Similar to almond paste, however, is not as strong in flavour, has a finer consistency and is more pliable. Cheaper brands often use ground apricot kernels and sugar.

MILK we use full-cream homogenised milk unless stated otherwise.

CARAMEL TOP 'N' FILL a canned milk product consisting of condensed milk that has been boiled to a caramel.

EVAPORATED unsweetened canned milk from which water has been extracted by evaporation; skim or low-fat varieties have 0.3% fat content.

FULL-CREAM POWDER instant powdered milk made from whole cow milk with liquid removed and emulsifiers added.

SWEETENED CONDENSED a canned milk product consisting of milk with more than half the water content removed and sugar added to the remaining milk.

MIXED DRIED FRUIT a combination of sultanas, raisins, currants, mixed peel and cherries.

MIXED PEEL candied citrus peel.

MIXED SPICE a classic spice mixture generally containing caraway, allspice, coriander, cumin, nutmeg and ginger, although cinnamon and other spices can be added. It is used with fruit and in cakes.

MOLASSES a thick, dark brown syrup, the residue from the refining of sugar; available in light, dark and blackstrap varieties. Its slightly bitter taste is an essential ingredient in American cooking, found in foods such as gingerbread, shoofly pie and boston baked beans.

MUESLI also known as granola; a combination of grains (mainly oats), nuts and dried fruits. Some manufacturers toast their product in oil and honey, adding crispness and kilojoules.

MUSLIN inexpensive, undyed, finely woven cotton fabric called for in cooking to strain stocks and sauces.

NUTMEG a strong and pungent spice ground from the dried nut of an evergreen tree native to Indonesia. Usually found ground but the flavour is more intense from a whole nut, available from spice shops, so it's best to grate your own. Used most often in baking and milk-based desserts, but also works nicely in savoury dishes. It is an ingredient in mixed spice mixtures.

OIL

COOKING SPRAY we use a cholesterol-free cooking spray made from canola oil.

OLIVE made from ripened olives. Extra virgin and virgin are the first and second press, respectively, of the olives and are therefore considered the best; the "extra light" or "light" name on other types refers to taste not fat levels.

PEANUT pressed from ground peanuts; most commonly used oil in Asian cooking because of its high smoke point (capacity to handle high heat without burning).

SESAME roasted, crushed, white sesame seeds; a flavouring rather than a cooking medium

VEGETABLE any oils from plant rather than animal fats.

ORANGE FLOWER WATER concentrated flavouring made from orange blossoms.

PASTRY

FILLO paper-thin sheets of raw pastry; brush each sheet with oil or melted butter, stack in layers, then cut and fold as directed.

SHEETS ready-rolled packaged sheets of frozen puff and shortcrust pastry, available from supermarkets.

PEANUTS also known as groundnut, not in fact a nut but the pod of a legume. We mainly use raw (unroasted) or unsalted roasted peanuts.

PEARL SUGAR see Sugar

PECANS native to the US and now grown locally; pecans are golden brown, buttery and rich. Good in savoury as well as sweet dishes; walnuts are a good substitute.

PEPITAS (PUMPKIN SEEDS) are the pale green kernels of dried pumpkin seeds; they can be bought plain or salted.

PERSIAN FAIRY FLOSS also sold as pashmak, is a form of fairy floss made from sesame and sugar. It has a different texture and its strands are said to resemble sheep's wool (pashmak in Persian means little wool). It is available from specialist food stores, some delicatessens and cake decorating suppliers.

PINE NUTS also called pignoli; not a nut but a small, cream-coloured kernel from pine cones. They are best roasted before use to bring out the flavour.

PISTACHIOS green, delicately flavoured nuts inside hard off-white shells. Available salted or unsalted in their shells; you can also get them shelled.

POLENTA also called cornmeal; a flour-like cereal of dried corn (maize). Also the dish made from it.

POMEGRANATE dark-red, leathery-skinned fresh fruit about the size of an orange filled with hundreds of seeds, each wrapped in an edible lucent-crimson pulp having a unique tangy sweet-sour flavour.

POPPY SEEDS small, dried, bluish-grey seeds of the poppy plant, with a crunchy texture and a nutty flavour. Can be purchased whole or ground in delicatessens and most supermarkets.

PRESERVED LEMON whole or quartered salted lemons preserved in a mixture of water, lemon juice, or olive oil, and occasionally with spices such as cinnamon, coriander and cloves. Use the rind only and rinse well under cold water before using.

QUINCE yellow-skinned fruit with a hard texture and an astringent, tart taste; eaten cooked or as a preserve. Long, slow cooking makes the flesh a deep rose pink.

RAISINS dried sweet grapes (traditionally muscatel grapes).

RHUBARB a plant with long, green-red stalks; becomes sweet and edible when cooked.

ROASTING/TOASTING nuts and dried coconut can be roasted in the oven to restore their fresh flavour and release their aromatic essential oils. Spread them evenly onto an oven tray then roast in a moderate oven for about 5 minutes. Desiccated coconut, pine nuts and

sesame seeds roast more evenly if stirred over low heat in a heavy-based frying pan; their natural oils will help turn them golden brown.
ROLLED OATS flattened oat grain rolled into flakes and traditionally used for porridge. Instant oats are also available, but use traditional oats for baking.
ROSEWATER extract made from crushed rose petals, called gulab in India; used for its aromatic quality in many sweetmeats and desserts.
SAFFRON stigma of a member of the crocus family, available ground or in strands; imparts a yellow-orange colour to food once infused. The quality can vary greatly; the best is the most expensive spice in the world.
SANDING SUGAR see Sugar
SEGMENTING a cooking term to describe cutting citrus fruits in such a way that pieces contain no pith, seed or membrane. The peeled fruit is cut towards the centre inside each membrane, forming wedges.
SEMOLINA coarsely ground flour milled from durum wheat; the flour used in making gnocchi, pasta and couscous.
SESAME SEEDS black and white are the most common of this small oval seed, however there are also red and brown varieties. The seeds are used in cuisines the world over as an ingredient and as a condiment. Roast the seeds in a heavy-based frying pan over low heat.
SHERRY fortified wine consumed as an aperitif or used in cooking. Sherries differ in colour and flavour; sold as fino (light, dry), amontillado (medium sweet, dark) and oloroso (full-bodied, very dark).
STAR ANISE dried star-shaped pod with an astringent aniseed flavour; used to flavour stocks and marinades. Available whole and ground.
SUGAR
BROWN a soft, finely granulated sugar retaining molasses for its characteristic colour and flavour.
CASTER (SUPERFINE) finely granulated table sugar.
DEMERARA small-grained golden-coloured crystal sugar.
ICING (CONFECTIONERS') also called powdered sugar; pulverised granulated sugar crushed together with a small amount of cornflour.
PEARL a coarse white sugar that keeps its shape when heated or exposed to moisture; it's available at specialist food and cake decorating stores.
PURE ICING (CONFECTIONERS') also known as powdered sugar.
SANDING a coloured decorating sugar that adds sparkle and colour to cakes, cupcakes and biscuits. This medium-sized crystal keeps its shape and colour after baking. It is available in a range of colours from specialist food and cake decorating stores.
RAW natural brown granulated sugar.
VANILLA available in supermarkets, usually with the spices. Or, you can make your own by putting a couple of vanilla beans in a jar of caster sugar.
WHITE (GRANULATED) coarse, granulated table sugar, also known as crystal sugar.
SULTANAS also called golden raisins; dried seedless white grapes.
TREACLE thick, dark syrup not unlike molasses; a by-product of sugar refining.
VANILLA
BEAN dried, long, thin pod from a tropical golden orchid; the minuscule black seeds inside the bean are used to impart a luscious vanilla flavour in baking and desserts. Place a whole bean in a jar of sugar to make vanilla sugar; a bean can be used three or four times.
EXTRACT made by extracting the flavour from the vanilla bean pod; pods are soaked, usually in alcohol, to capture the authentic flavour.
PASTE made from vanilla pods and contains real seeds. Is highly concentrated – 1 teaspoon replaces a whole vanilla pod. Found in most supermarkets in the baking section.
VINEGAR, WHITE made from the spirit of cane sugar.
WAFFLES true belgian waffles are made from a yeast dough; each waffle is sprinkled with sugar, resulting in a crisp, rich product with a slightly caramelised flavour. Available from large supermarket or delicatessens.
WALNUTS as well as being a good source of fibre and healthy oils, nuts contain a range of vitamins, minerals and other beneficial plant components called phytochemicals. Walnuts contain the beneficial omega-3 fatty acids.
YEAST (dried and fresh) raising agent used in dough making. Granular (7g sachets) and fresh compressed (20g blocks) yeast can almost always be substituted one for the other when yeast is called for.
YOGHURT we use plain full-cream yoghurt unless stated otherwise.
ZESTING TOOL also known as a zester; has tiny, sharp-edged holes across its end so that, as you press it into the rind of any citrus fruit and draw it towards you, it cuts fine shreds from the zest without removing any of the bitter white pith underneath.

CONVERSION CHART

MEASURES

One Australian metric measuring cup holds approximately 250ml; one Australian metric tablespoon holds 20ml; one Australian metric teaspoon holds 5ml.

The difference between one country's measuring cups and another's is within a two- or three-teaspoon variance, and will not affect your cooking results. North America, New Zealand and the United Kingdom use a 15ml tablespoon.

All cup and spoon measurements are level. The most accurate way of measuring dry ingredients is to weigh them. When measuring liquids, use a clear glass or plastic jug with the metric markings.

We use large eggs with an average weight of 60g.

DRY MEASURES

METRIC	IMPERIAL
15g	½oz
30g	1oz
60g	2oz
90g	3oz
125g	4oz (¼lb)
155g	5oz
185g	6oz
220g	7oz
250g	8oz (½lb)
280g	9oz
315g	10oz
345g	11oz
375g	12oz (¾lb)
410g	13oz
440g	14oz
470g	15oz
500g	16oz (1lb)
750g	24oz (1½lb)
1kg	32oz (2lb)

LIQUID MEASURES

METRIC	IMPERIAL
30ml	1 fluid oz
60ml	2 fluid oz
100ml	3 fluid oz
125ml	4 fluid oz
150ml	5 fluid oz
190ml	6 fluid oz
250ml	8 fluid oz
300ml	10 fluid oz
500ml	16 fluid oz
600ml	20 fluid oz
1000ml (1 litre)	1¾ pints

LENGTH MEASURES

METRIC	IMPERIAL
3mm	⅛in
6mm	¼in
1cm	½in
2cm	¾in
2.5cm	1in
5cm	2in
6cm	2½in
8cm	3in
10cm	4in
13cm	5in
15cm	6in
18cm	7in
20cm	8in
22cm	9in
25cm	10in
28cm	11in
30cm	12in (1ft)

OVEN TEMPERATURES

The oven temperatures in this book are for conventional ovens; if you have a fan-forced oven, decrease the temperature by 10-20 degrees.

	°C (Celsius)	°F (Fahrenheit)
Very slow	120	250
Slow	150	300
Moderately slow	160	325
Moderate	180	350
Moderately hot	200	400
Hot	220	425
Very hot	240	475

The imperial measurements used in these recipes are approximate only. Measurements for cake pans are approximate only. Using same-shaped cake pans of a similar size should not affect the outcome of your baking. We measure the inside top of the cake pan to determine sizes.

INDEX

INDEX

E

F

INDEX

BAUER

This book is published in 2015 by Octopus Publishing Group Limited
based on materials licensed to it by Bauer Media Books, Australia
Bauer Media Books are published by Bauer Media Pty Limited
54 Park St, Sydney; GPO Box 4088, Sydney, NSW 2001 Australia
phone +61 2 9282 8618; fax +61 2 9126 3702
www.awwcookbooks.com.au

BAUER MEDIA BOOKS
Publisher JO RUNCIMAN
Editorial & food director PAMELA CLARK
Director of sales, marketing & rights BRIAN CEARNES
Art director & designer HANNAH BLACKMORE
Senior editor STEPHANIE KISTNER
Food editor EMMA BRAZ
Operations manager DAVID SCOTTO

A catalogue record for this book is available from the British Library.
ISBN: 978-1-74245-606-5
© Bauer Media Pty Limited 2015
ABN 18 053 273 546
*This publication is copyright.
No part of it may be reproduced or transmitted in any form without the written permission of the publishers.*

Published and distributed in the United Kingdom by
OCTOPUS PUBLISHING GROUP
Carmelite House
50 Victoria Embankment
London, EC4Y 0DZ
United Kingdom
info@octopus-publishing.co.uk
www.octopusbooks.co.uk

Printed in China with 1010 Printing Pty Limited.

INTERNATIONAL FOREIGN LANGUAGE RIGHTS
Brian Cearnes, Bauer Media Books
bcearnes@bauer-media.com.au